CULTURE SHOCK!

A Survival Guide to Customs and Etiquette

MELBOURNE

Ruth Rajasingam

Marshall Cavendish
Editions

Published by Marshall Cavendish Editions
An imprint of Marshall Cavendish International

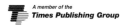

A member of the
Times Publishing Group

Other Marshall Cavendish Offices:
Marshall Cavendish Corporation. 99 White Plains Road, Tarrytown NY 10591–9001, USA • Marshall Cavendish International (Thailand) Co Ltd. 253 Asoke, 12th Flr, Sukhumvit 21 Road, Klongtoey Nua, Wattana, Bangkok 10110, Thailand • Marshall Cavendish (Malaysia) Sdn Bhd, Times Subang, Lot 46, Subang Hi-Tech Industrial Park, Batu Tiga, 40000 Shah Alam, Selangor Darul Ehsan, Malaysia.

Marshall Cavendish is a registered trademark of Times Publishing Limited

National Library Board, Singapore Cataloguing-in-Publication Data

Name(s): Rajasingam, Ruth.
Title: CultureShock! Melbourne : a survival guide to customs and etiquette / Ruth Rajasingam.
Other title(s): Melbourne : a survival guide to customs and etiquette | Culture shock Melbourne
Description: Singapore : Marshall Cavendish Editions, [2018] | Series: Culture shock!
Identifier(s): OCN 1065533720 | ISBN 978-981-4828-17-8 (paperback)
Subject(s): LCSH: Etiquette--Australia--Melbourne (Vic.). | Melbourne (Vic.)--Social life and customs. | Melbourne (Vic.)--Description and travel.
Classification: DDC 994.51--dc23

All illustrations by TRIGG

All photos by the author except on pages vi (Nate Watson on Unsplash.com); 18 (Joseph Kelly on Unsplash.com); 111 (Steven Groeneveld on Unsplash.com); and 142 (Lucile Noiriel on Unsplash.com).

Printed in Singapore

ABOUT THE SERIES

Culture shock is a state of disorientation that can come over anyone who has been thrust into unknown surroundings, away from one's comfort zone. *CultureShock!* is a series of trusted and reputed guides which has, for decades, been helping expatriates and long-term visitors to cushion the impact of culture shock whenever they move to a new country.

Written by people who have lived in the country and experienced culture shock themselves, these books provide all the information necessary for anyone to cope with these feelings of disorientation more effectively. The guides are written in a style that is easy to read and cover a range of topics that will give readers enough advice, hints and tips to make their lives as normal as possible again.

Each book is structured in the same manner. It begins with the first impressions that visitors will have of that city or country. To understand a culture, one must first understand the people—where they came from, who they are, the values and traditions they live by, as well as their customs and etiquette. This is covered in the first half of the book.

Then on with the practical aspects—how to settle in with the greatest of ease. Authors walk readers through topics such as how to find accommodation, get the utilities and telecommunications up and running, enrol the children in school and keep in the pink of health. But that's not all. Once the essentials are out of the way, venture out and try the food, enjoy more of the culture and travel to other areas. Then be immersed in the language of the country before discovering more about the business side of things.

To round off, snippets of basic information are offered before readers are 'tested' on customs and etiquette of the country. Useful words and phrases, a comprehensive resource guide and list of books for further research are also included for easy reference.

CONTENTS

The famous domed ceiling at the La Trobe Reading Room of the State Library Victoria

ACKNOWLEDGEMENTS

My humble and heartfelt gratitude to my family, friends and acquaintances who have contributed to this book, both directly and indirectly. In writing about Melbourne, I have also relied on literature by Australian authors whose names are listed in the Further Reading list, as well as publicly available information on government websites and newsites. Any errors, omissions and misinterpretations are mine and I apologise for these.

In particular I would like to express my deep gratitude to my husband Ganesh without whose patience and support, I would not have completed the writing, as well as my children, Dinesh and Shirahni.

Soli Deo Gloria.

Pedestrian bridge over the Yarra River with view of the cityscape in the background

PREFACE

Melbourne has a reputation to maintain. Named the world's most liveable city for seven years in a row since 2011 by the Economist Intelligence Unit, Melbourne is among 140 cities to receive a perfect score for healthcare, education and infrastructure. Other factors considered are a city's stability, culture and environment. While the report's target audience is corporate executives and their families relocating overseas, Melbourne remains a charming city to be experienced whether you are a business traveller, student, tourist or long-term resident.

The usual questions of one new to a city—Where to live? Where to eat? What is the best mode of transportation? What's on this weekend?—are easily answered. Melbourne is a relatively easy city to adapt to and welcomes all types of visitors. Everyday encounters with Melburnians will reveal how cosmopolitan this city is as it is home to people from more than 200 nationalities.

Melbourne has championed multiculturalism successfully over the past years. While there have been recent calls to stem the flow of migration due to the challenges to the city's infrastructure, such as housing and traffic, it remains a civic city, which tries to meet the needs of its local community. Urban historian Graeme Davison has said that "one of the threads through its history has been a quaint sense of civic values; an idea of a shared purpose beyond commerce and getting ahead".

The information and insights I have tried to provide are limited to my stay in this city. However I have sought the views of many who have called Melbourne home for more than a quarter of a century as well as new residents, students and business travellers. These provide different perspectives to the people and life in this city. I hope that it will offer a good background to explore and experience the richness this city has to offer.

FIRST IMPRESSIONS

❮This will be a place for a village.❯

— John Batman, Australian explorer

First impressions count. Wisdom, however, dictates that impressions invariably change with time. My first impression of Melbourne was in 1989, when I visited the city to decide if I'd like to pursue postgraduate studies here. I remember walking down the Yarra River, visiting Flagstaff gardens and thinking to myself what a tranquil and beautiful city it was. It reminded me of Britain. As things turned out, however, I did not pursue my studies then but several years later.

More recently, as I landed again at the Melbourne International Airport at Tullamarine and made my way through the crowds of passengers, the first thing I noticed was how ethnically diverse the passengers were. I was excited to see people from all over the world. The scene outside the gates was touching as passengers were greeted by friends and family with hugs, kisses and flowers—reminiscent of villagers greeting their loved ones after a long separation. Melbourne is very much the multicultural new world.

While the immigration process was reasonably efficient, the airport lacked the numerous facilities of a modern airport such as Singapore's Changi International Airport. I had some trepidation over customs declaration, having heard of horror stories from other travellers into Australia and the long interrogation sessions I had seen on the cable television programme, *Border Security*. I had been reassured by relatives from Australia that as long as I honestly declared what I was carrying, there will not be any problems. Luckily, I had nothing from the list of prohibited goods—such as fresh fruits, vegetables and some dairy products—and getting through customs was a breeze.

The classic view of Princes Bridge with the Melbourne city skyline in the background.

CITY CENTRE

What awaited me along the drive to the city was unexciting. There was no train or subway to the city centre, unlike in other big cities. While there are plans in the works to develop a train route from the airport to the city centre, the only travel options in the meantime are taxis, Ubers, Skybuses, families or friends. The scenery was flat with industrial buildings and a long stretch of road along the Tullamarine freeway. As I passed the green belt of Parkville, I noticed the changing landscape as the old gave way to the new. On one side was the University of Melbourne but as I drove into the city, I began to notice the outline of skyscrapers.

Architectural gems were aplenty and quaint trams glided through the crowded city of cosy cafés and interesting artworks. There was a laid-back feel to the city: Office workers in workwear shared the city streets with students in casual attire, tourists and mothers with children in tow.

St Paul's Cathedral

The iconic Flinders Street Station

At one end of the city was the famous Flinders Street railway station. Built in 1910, it was still the gathering place of all commuters who "meet under the clocks". The grand red brick and golden yellow stucco building built in an Edwardian baroque style saw thousands of commuters passing through its doors daily. Just behind Flinders Street Station was the South Bank, right by the Yarra River, the main river running through Melbourne. Many crossed the bridge to get to the Melbourne Arts Centre and the National Gallery of Victoria.

Just opposite Flinders Street Station, at Federation Square, was the Melbourne Visitors Centre, a good stop for the first-time visitor to the city. The glass enclave was easy to find and friendly staff took the time to find out what my interests were, arming me with the necessary information and options for things to do such as volunteer-led walking tours.

With Melbourne being Australia's coffee capital, I decided

Pedestrian Bridge at Southgate

to try a coffee. My first stop was the Queen Victoria Market, for coffee and food. The old market, a popular destination for tourists and locals, sold not only fresh produce, meats and seafood, but knick knacks, souvenirs and cooked food. I tasted my first few sips of a flat white (an Australian invention of espresso and milk), and it was truly one of the best coffees I had ever tasted. My appetite was whet by the variety of breakfast options from hot jam doughnuts and croissants to sourdough bread and Turkish borek!

The fresh market boasted European-style deli foods such as cheeses and dried fruits, and also fresh seafood and red meats. It was obvious that the availability of fresh food at affordable prices was a major draw for living in this city. Ready-to-eat food available at the food court ranged from Sri Lankan curries to American-style burgers to Cantonese-Malaysian stir-fries. The variety of foods was testament to the diverse cultures found in Melbourne, which was truly a melting pot.

Once I was ready to explore the city, it was easy getting directions from the friendly locals. I pondered my many options—walk along the Yarra River, stroll in the Botanic Gardens, join a walking tour of the city, or admire the architecture of old buildings? I decided on the easy option and made my way to the city centre where I hopped on the free tourist tram which took passengers past the major tourist attractions in a circular route.

The city was well planned with wide roads in a grid. Old buildings added to the city's old-world European charm. I saw the hidden laneways and made a mental note to discover them on another day. Japanese eateries, sushi bars, ramen houses, Chinese and Indian restaurants dotted the route. Traffic appeared heavy with trams running down the middle of the road, cars galore and pedestrians everywhere.

Melbourne's Trams

Trams were introduced to Australia in 1885 when the first tram cars were imported from the United States. These could only accommodate 22 seated and 34 standing passengers. Electric trams were introduced in 1889 and by 1916, the trams carried more than a million passengers. While most Australian cities discontinued the use of trams, Melbourne went against the trend to update and refurbish their existing ones. The W class tram which operates today has become a Melburnian icon.

ST KILDA

I took a tram to St Kilda, an area famous for its beach and a family-themed amusement park, Luna Park. St Kilda used to be infamous for being a hangout for druggies but has since been gentrified and turned into the perfect place for families to spend a day out at the beach. It seemed chilly for spring but I decided to walk along the beach and made my way towards the pier to look out at the wide expanse of water. It was a peaceful place with birds chirping in the air and ice-cream or a coffee available at the kiosk. Penguins would form a parade at dusk and many locals and tourists would flock to see them. Another thing to experience in

Melbourne was the Sunday market on the beach boasting more than a hundred stalls selling locally-designed creations like jewellery and hats.

Luna Park was instantly recognisable for its iconic white roller coaster that stood out in the skyline. Built in 1912, it was still popular among families with children. Entry was free and you only paid for the rides. After asking around, I was directed to one of the popular European cake shops with a tantalising window display on Acland Street. This was the famous Monarch Cakes, a Polish cake shop which served an authentic cherry slice and chocolate *kugelhoupf*, perfect for my sweet tooth, in a cosy and quaint 1950s setting. I stayed there for a while—there was too much to discover for one day at St Kilda.

Soon, the weather would change; even then the winds on the beach seemed cold for spring. After all, this was Melbourne with its unpredictable weather; I had been warned that it was possible to experience four seasons in a day. The best way to dress was to layer what you wore so that the extra layers could be removed as the weather warmed up.

Luna Park and its iconic roller coaster

TRAFFIC AND DENSITY

As I made my way back home, I found myself stuck in the middle of peak hour traffic. It reminded me of Singapore but somehow worse, because Melbourne was a bigger city and everything was bigger, wider and more spread out. As the world's most liveable city, Melbourne had a burgeoning population. Many chose to drive to work and only slightly more than 10 per cent of the population used public transport. According to a 2017 report by the Grattan Institute, more than 1.3 million people, or 74 per cent of the people in Greater Melbourne, relied solely on cars to get to work.

To address the problem of traffic congestion in the city, the state government started many projects such as the Melbourne Metro Tunnel (set to boost rail patronage by 39,000 people by running three of the busiest lines through a new tunnel); a new toll road for commuters on the West Gate Bridge; and the West Gate Tunnel, a 5-km toll road. Gone were the days when you could enjoy driving the freeways free of traffic. You now had to plan your route in advance and choose a good time to set off to avoid traffic jams.

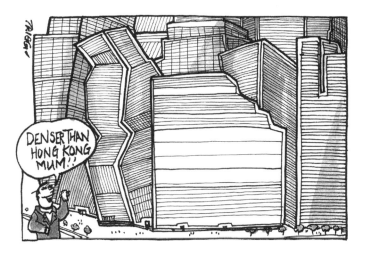

The increasing density of the city came hand in hand with increasing wealth, population diversity and changing lifestyles. The Centre for Urban Transitions in September 2016 surveyed 2,000 Sydney and Melbourne households in established middle-ring suburbs and found that only 60 per cent of residents wished to live in a detached house and yard, a 30 per cent decrease from the 1990s. This survey postulated that the new generation of Australians have moved on from the Aussie dream of living in a huge detached house and yard to higher-density living. This change may be fuelled by pragmatic considerations such as access to good public transport, jobs and services.

Melbourne's Central Business District (CBD) has been found to be Australia's most densely populated region and is largely made up of international students renting apartments. It has been reported that 77 per cent of the people living in the CBD have both parents born overseas—a changing demographic for the city.

Critics of the building boom in the city may be justified as there have been studies which show that high rise apartment towers built in central Melbourne may be four times the maximum density allowed in other crowded cities such as Hong Kong, New York and Tokyo. Here too, part of the attraction to inner-city high rise living may be access to amenities and work.

With the rise in demand for housing, Melbourne's boundaries have extended and housing prices in suburbs up to 100 km from the city centre have increased. Many have predicted and hoped that the market will correct itself (which is slowly occurring) but for a newcomer to Melbourne intending to buy or rent property, the best advice is to come prepared with your own finances. There are restrictions to obtaining loans without a history of work in Melbourne.

TRANSFORMING A CITY

The city centre in Melbourne today is alive at night. Its laneways are bustling with bars, restaurants and street artists. Cyclists, pedestrians and trams contribute to this vibrant scene. This is in sharp contrast to the city in 1989, which was quiet and dead past office hours. Much of Melbourne's rejuvenation was due to careful urban planning. In 1993, Dutch architect Jan Gehl, a visiting professor with the University of Melbourne, after spending countless hours walking the streets and imagining what could be done to bring life to them, worked with the City of Melbourne and recommended creating spaces for outdoor dining, much like European cities such as Paris and Rome. This idea has born fruit and today the city buzzes with outdoor cafés, decorated laneways and pedestrians swarming the streets.

The previous state governments, too, have contributed to this change. Housing projects in the CBD have increased by the thousands since the 1990s, catapulting the city's transformation. Licensing laws were changed, thanks to

recommendations of the Nieuwenhuysen Report on liquor licensing in 1986, allowing people to order a drink without first ordering a whole meal. The reforms were intended to create an urbane, liberalised culture of drinking in the city. To break the hotels' monopoly over the sale and service of liquor, small bars could now be set up and a separate small bar liquor licence was created.

Big building projects such as the construction of Crown Casino and high rise apartment buildings in the city, and increased small retail spaces in the city for businesses have contributed significantly to the city's urban renewal process. Changes to the education policy and residency requirements have led to the building of new housing in the city and this has led in turn to the increase in number of people flocking to live in Melbourne both on short- and long-term bases.

These developments have been met with mixed reactions. There are those who lament the rude changes to the city as more people and construction sites appear, while there are those who are happy that the economy has turned around thanks to more jobs being created to meet the demands of this influx of people. In particular, the hospitality and education sectors have benefitted. Many more tourists are flocking to enjoy what the city has to offer; restaurants, museums, laneways and attractions are always filled with tourists.

Meyers Place, located off Bourke Street, was a popular watering hole for twenty years until it closed its doors in June 2017. It was a good example of a dramatic transformation from a dilapidated warehouse to the city's oldest laneway bar. Opened in 1994, Meyers Place was widely credited as the first laneway bar in Melbourne, had received a number of awards and was inducted into the Eat Drink Design Awards Hall of Fame in 2014, as a model for small bar and laneway culture.

HOMELESSNESS AND
AFFORDABLE HOUSING

To see so many homeless people on the streets in the world's most liveable city is sad. Homeless people in Melbourne, like so many modern cities, drive home the point that there are those less fortunate who have fallen through the cracks. The state government has spent an estimated A$194 million a year to address this problem, but it still persists.

The longer life spans of parents (leading to a deferred passing of property to children); foreign investment and speculation in the property market; the rising cost of living which has not kept abreast with wage growth, have all contributed to the housing problem. There is a need for the government to step in and facilitate the construction of more housing for the lower end of the market, a demographic unable to afford the traditionally affordable Melbourne suburbs. The issue is exacerbated by multiple factors including mental illness, family conflict and drug addiction.

According to an article in the *Sydney Morning Herald* on 15 February 2017, affordable housing remains a big issue in Melbourne today. I have witnessed this in my neighbourhood. The influx of migrants with new wealth has led to soaring house prices and resentment, especially young people who are trying to buy their first home. The median home price in 2011 was about A$600,000; in six years it almost doubled to A$900,000.

Homelessness is not only a problem in the city but in the suburbs. The statistics, if to be believed, are a cause for worry. Private rentals are expensive, shared accommodation is often full, cheap motels are only a short-term fix and the waiting list for public housing is only getting longer. According to an ABC report, the Salvation Army's Sunshine office in western Melbourne sees a queue of up to 40 people daily for food vouchers and accommodation.

The Council to Homeless Persons has reported that getting help in suburban and regional areas is harder than in the CBD, where there is a greater concentration of support services. The organisation came up with a A$7.5 million plan to deploy teams of 12 outreach workers to five homelessness hotspots in Victoria: Frankston, Dandenong, Broadmeadows, Sunshine and Shepparton. According to the Australian Bureau of Statistics, the rate of homelessness in Australia has increased 4.6 per cent over the last five years before 2016; more than 116,000 people are homeless in Australia, representing 50 homeless persons for every 10,000.

Another angle to this problem is the crisis Melbourne is facing with the availability of public housing in Victoria, exacerbated by the population growth. Older Australians' constant worry seems to be the affordability of housing for their children and their children's families. State government figures show there are currently more than 35,000 Victorians waiting for public housing, and welfare agencies have pushed the government to invest in public housing. The Urban Development Institute of Australia (UDIA) has declared that Victoria is underprepared for its booming population and needs to embrace higher density living if it is to keep up with demand for new homes. According to them, in spite of record-high levels of housing development, the state had a shortfall of 9,000 new properties in the past two years. The model of fringe housing—building homes up to 50 km outside Melbourne city—provide some relief as there are house-and-land packages which sell for less than A$800,000. However, this raises the additional problem of the long commutes that these residents have to make to get to the city for work.

The issue is not hopeless and there are attempts to resolve this. Fortunately, in Melbourne, there are many welfare organisations that try to help with the problem of homelessness. The Victorian government has a Public Housing Renewal Program where old public housing blocks are demolished and replaced with tall, higher-density developments containing a mix of public and private housing.

SUBURBAN LIFE

Suburban life is a feature that remains a hallmark of Melbourne: houses with backyards, a park where people walk their dogs and children play, the neighbourhood milk bar, shopping strips, a nearby shopping mall with amenities, people exercising and working in the garden in the warmer months. It all reminds me of the Australian movie, *The Castle,* where a typical working class Melbourne family fought to retain and remain in their house when the government and airport authorities had plans to demolish the house. In Melbourne you will see that a man's home is his castle.

In general, some things have changed in Melbourne. There are less peaceful and natural green spaces than before. Children don't walk to school these days but get driven. Yet there is still much to love in this global village. I love the open spaces, the unending roads, blue skies and the bright sunshine which sometimes pierces the eyes. Walking around my neighbourhood one night, I saw a few possums hanging upside down from the electricity cables, which run along some neighbourhoods. I stared hard, thinking it resembled a furry big cat. There are two types of possums that you may see in Melbourne, the ringtail possum and the common brush tail possum. They rest during the day but come out at night, eating the leaves, flowers and fruits of many native and exotic trees and shrubs in suburban gardens. You may hear them walking on roofs in the night but you should just leave them be unless they decide to build a nest in your roof. Possums are protected under the Wildlife Act and they are regulations to be followed if you wish to trap them.

Besides possums, other traces of nature coming into the suburbs are the sounds of birds chirping in your backyard. You may be awoken in the morning by the chirping and warbling of magpies. While they are generally not harmful, I have learnt that magpies may be a nuisance between August and November, the breeding season when they become aggressive and sometimes attack passers-by. Sparrows and colourful rainbow lorikeets with their red beaks, orange breasts and green wings complete the picture.

The charm of the city with its trams, old and new buildings, laneways, the open spaces and nature—they are all part of what makes Melbourne one of the world's most attractive, beautiful and liveable cities.

CHAPTER 2

LAND AND HISTORY

GEOGRAPHY

From its humble beginnings as the site for a settlement by the Yarra River chosen by entrepreneur John Batman in 1835, Melbourne has grown considerably. Today Melbourne stretches across an area of alpine forests, the Yarra River, the Dandenong Ranges in the east and the Macedon Ranges in the west. Spanning approximately 8,694 sq km (3,356 sq mi) it is the capital city of Victoria and is located at the head of the Port Phillip Bay on the south-eastern coast.

Melbourne boasts a varied topography from bayside beaches located in the south eastern suburbs such as Port Melbourne and Albert Park to surf beaches in Sorrento and Portsea to hills such as the Macedon Ranges and You

Pier at St Kilda

Yangs ridge to bushland valleys such as Merri Creek and Darebin Creek.

Melbourne's population today is over 4.5 million which accounts for 19.05 per cent of the national population. It is the second most populated state in Australia after Sydney. Unlike other Australia cities which were penal settlements, Melbourne stands alone as being the only city founded by enterprise: the city was made up of free citizens. Today there are more than 140 ethnic groups living in Melbourne.

HISTORY

Some 40,000 years ago and long before any Europeans settled in Melbourne, Melbourne was home to the native Kulin nation, comprising the Wurundjeri, Boonerwrung, Taungurong, Djadjawurrung and Wathaurung peoples. These peoples eked out a living by hunting for waterfowl, eating shellfish from the coast and gathering food from the landscape. They lived off the land, making clothes from possum skins. Archaeological digs unearthed a skull believed to be about 15,000 years old, before the last Ice Age when Tasmania was still a part of the continent. However, the ecological changes brought rising water levels and the lifestyle of the locals was more rudely disrupted by smallpox epidemics in the 1790s and 1830s when foreign sealers and whalers brought this disease with them. The toll on the local population was tragically heavy and their numbers dwindled to a quarter of what it was before.

It is widely believed that it was John Batman, a Tasmanian businessman who signed a treaty with the local Wurundjeri chiefs on 6 June 1835 to purchase the site near Northcote, and became Melbourne's founder. Unfortunately this treaty was cancelled by the government of the day as they declared the land *terra nullius*. In the meantime, another Tasmanian adventurer John Fawkner and his party of settlers arrived in Melbourne also in 1835, thus giving rise to claims that Fawkner may have also founded Melbourne. Be that as it may, it was Batman who stopped at the mouth of the Yarra River on 8 June 1835, declaring it a good site for a village. Melbourne at that time was not a town and the two groups of sellers lived at different sites quite amicably.

Terra Nullius

Terra nullius is a Latin expression which is a legal term meaning land belonging to no one. It is an international law principle that allows a state to occupy land. This allowed the English authorities to proclaim Melbourne *terra nullius* and deny the Aboriginal people rights to the land. Therefore the Aboriginal people could not sell or assign land, and no one could acquire the land except through the Crown.

For the British authorities, it was undoubtedly a good site for settlement. There was a rise in the number of settlers within a year and by 1837, there were 400 settlers living in tents, huts and weatherboard homes. Order was established by police magistrate William Lonsdale in 1836. In 1837, Melbourne was given its name, after a British Prime Minister, William Lamb, second Viscount Melbourne of Kilmore. Interestingly some of its previous names were Batmania, Bearbrass and Birrarung. Much of what you see in the city centre can be credited to able administration of the early governors. In 1837 Governor Bourke assigned Robert Hoddle the Assistant Surveyor General to plan the sale of land. Hoddle created the grid road system which modern Melbourne enjoys. These wide streamlined streets impress every visitor as they give the city a sense of grandeur. However Hoddle had to compromise on the wide streets by having little lanes which today are a hallmark of Melbourne city with its cultural and social spaces.

The city saw some hard times, experiencing an economic downturn in the 1840s and a crash in 1942. Melbourne was declared a city by Queen Victoria in June 1847 and this created a short building boom. The city was developed with housing in the inner city areas of Flinders Street to Collins Street and King Street to Elizabeth Street, with brick houses, pubs, hotels and the basic amenities such as a bakery, butcher, chemist, tailor, bank and post office. However, the population growth was not in tandem with infrastructure such as roads and other facilities. Despite this, most Melburnians enjoyed a better quality of life, although there were victims to this growth: the Aboriginals, who languished with diseases and displacement. On 1 July 1851, Port Philip District (Victoria) was formally recognised as a separate state.

BOOM AND BUST

The city, however, flourished from 1851 to 1859 when gold was discovered at Buninyong near Bendigo and Ballarat which is about 160 km away from Melbourne. This caused a surge in the population as many adventurers came in search of a fortune. It was not only Europeans who came;

some of the early adventurers were Chinese. The railway was extended to the gold mining towns but there were challenges to other sectors such as health, housing and water supply due to the burgeoning population.

This was a period when many iconic buildings were built. The University of Melbourne, the State Library and the Young and Jackson hotel were but some of them. The Exhibition Building built in 1854 and designed by Joseph Reed attracted exhibits from Europe and the USA. These boom years saw the birth of the Melbourne Cup, a horse racing competition which is still an icon and more recently, a public holiday for all to enjoy in Melbourne.

Melbourne was Australia's most populous city in 1865. The iconic buildings we see today such as Melbourne Town Hall, the Supreme Court, The Royal Mint, St Patrick's Cathedral and Queen Victoria Market were built at this time. Elizabeth Ramsay-Laye, author of *Social Life and Manners in Australia*, wrote in 1861: "Melbourne was a stately city ... lavishing her gold on everything that will beautify or adorn her, and gives her a place among the cities of the Old World."

In 1885, Melbourne was one of the world's most populated cites, second only to London. It was also one of the wealthiest cities in the world and became popularly known as "Marvellous Melbourne", a phrase coined by British journalist George Sala. This period saw the development of suburban Melbourne where classes of society settled in different areas east, west and north of the city. Sadly the boom did not last and an economic depression affected the city's fortunes in the 1890s. This led to the collapse of many businesses and a drop in land value and unemployment. To help create jobs and boost the economy, a sewerage project was started in 1897 to resolve the city's air pollution and hygiene problems; open gutters carrying waste and manure had earned the city its nickname, "Smellbourne".

PARKS

Parks were seen as important in developing sport for its residents and promoting social harmony among the various classes of people. Charles Joseph La Trobe, Superintendent of the Port Phillip District and Victoria's first lieutenant-governor in 1854, was instrumental in reserving from sale large tracts of land, which included areas now occupied by Royal Park, Royal Botanic Gardens, Fitzroy Gardens and Carlton Gardens. In 1886 Frederick Law Olmsted, designer of New York's Central Park, included Melbourne, along with other cities such as Paris, Liverpool and San Francisco as those cities profoundly influenced in their development and way of life by the introduction of parks. The supply of water in 1957 with the construction of reservoirs enabled the setting up of ornamental gardens such as the Fitzroy and Carlton gardens, Flagstaff Gardens, Treasury Gardens and St Kilda Botanical Gardens. Most suburbs contained public parks and gardens by the end of the 19th century.

Port Phillip Bay was also developed for recreation with baths on its foreshore. Together with tennis courts, walking paths, piers and bandstands, Melburnians could enjoy exercise and be entertained.

Melbourne's first public playground was opened in Lincoln Square, Carlton by the Premier of Victoria in 1907. In 1976 the Premier inaugurated the Garden State Committee whose aim was to identify ways to improve, expand and protect private and public landscapes. This raised social awareness and has resulted in Victoria being referred to as the Garden State.

FEDERATION YEARS

The city slowly recovered from the economic depression and in the early 1900s, Melbourne became the federal capital when Australia became a commonwealth. It continued as Australia's capital until 1927 when Canberra was designed to

Dandenong Ranges Botanic Garden

be the capital city of Australia. This era saw the rise of electric trams, street lighting, theatres and cinema. Women earned their right to vote in 1908. However this recovery was impaired by World Wars I and II. There was massive unemployment too.

World War II brought Americans to Melbourne as US General Douglas Macarthur took up temporary residence in Melbourne, setting up his headquarters as Supreme Commander of Allied Forces in the South-West Pacific, before moving to Brisbane. The presence of the affluent American soldier caused some tension although their presence helped boost the economy.

The end of World War II saw the influx of migrants—there were now Jews, Italians, Greeks and Dutch in Melbourne and all over Australia. In 1951, Melbourne celebrated the Centenary of Victoria and the 50th anniversary of Federation in Australia with a theatre production, *An Aboriginal Moomba: Out of the Dark* and a festival over the Labour Day weekend with fireworks and carnivals. Melbourne hosted the Summer

Olympics in 1956 for the first time. By the 1950s, the Australian dream was being realised as families achieved their dream of owning a quarter acre suburban block and a Holden car. The earliest suburbs such as Carlton, Prahran and Brighton were built on streets of terrace houses with iron wrought verandas, a feature of inner city housing.

The city saw growth and an increase in diversity with different ethnicities bringing their culture and foods (for example, the Italians brought coffee) into Melbourne. Bourke

The Shrine of Remembrance

A memorial at The Shrine

R.A.A.F.

UNITED KINGDOM

EUROPE

ATLANTIC

MIDDLE EAST

EAST INDIES

S.E. ASIA

NEW GUINEA

S.W. PACIFIC

1939 - 45

Street was developed as a shopping strip for pedestrians and a new hub was born. Many other iconic buildings and districts were erected: the Rialto Building in 1986, the transformation of Southbank in the 1980s and 1990s with the Southgate Arts and Leisure Precinct and the Crown Casino in the 1990s.

THE ROAD TO MULTICULTURALISM

Melbourne-born historian and author of the *Tyranny of Distance* Geoffrey Blainey was known for his views against multiculturalism. It is widely acknowledged that Blainey had addressed a Rotary conference in the Victorian city of Warrnambool in 1984 where he expressed concern over the high level of migrants from Asia when there was already high unemployment, fearing it would cause tension. His controversial view was that the Australian government's immigration policy was increasingly being influenced by multicultural ideology to the detriment of the national interest and the majority of Australians. The controversy and widespread protests eventually led him to resign from his position as dean at the University of Melbourne a few years later. Yet today he is still regarded as a leading Australian historian and was awarded a Companion of the Order of Australia in 2000 for his contributions to academia, research and scholarship.

In contrast, the late Donald Horne, a public historian and recipient of the Order of Australia, had argued as early as in 1964 that Australia needed to be more serious about living with Asia and the country's future would hold dramatic possibilities.

More recently, the coalition government led by Malcolm Turnbull states definitively that Australia is defined "not by race, religion or culture" and that Australians look like every face, every race, every background.

MELBOURNE'S ARCADES

The arcades built in the Victorian era exude the old world charm of Melbourne. The Block Arcade situated on Collins Street has a range of eclectic shops. A notable presence is the Hopetoun Tea Room which has a tantalising window display of cakes and slices, tempting many a passerby, both locals and visitors. The Cathedral Arcade, located between Swanston Street and Flinders Lane, was built in 1925 in an Art Deco style with stained glass and arches.

The Royal Arcade, which links Bourke Street Mall, Little Collins Street and Elizabeth Street, is another Victorian gem known for its black-and-white tiled floors. It was designed by English architect Charles Webb, was the first arcade in Melbourne. There are two giant statues of Gog and Magog, mythological figures guarding the Gaunt's clock inside the arcade, that are modelled on similar figures found in the Guildhall, London in 1708.

SIGNIFICANT DATES
1835–1885

After its founding in 1835, there was an increased recognition of the city with Melbourne designated as the capital of the Port Phillip district, and subsequently made a legal, port and administrative centre. It was recognised by Queen Victoria as a city. The Royal Melbourne Hospital and the University of Melbourne were founded during this period.

There was much infrastructure development with the completion of the State Library of Victoria, the Melbourne Museum, and the Queen Victoria Market. Ned Kelly, a famous Australian bushranger was hanged in the Melbourne Gaol in 1880. The first cable tram line was opened.

1885–1935

The Commonwealth of Australia was formed with Melbourne

as its capital. A few notable firsts such as the first electric tram service, the first Australian Open championship, and the completion of Flinders Street station building.

1935–1985
During this period, the first parking meters were installed and the first television station was formed. The city loop was set up. Melbourne experienced a dust storm and the Ash Wednesday fires in 1983.

1985–2018
When it was opened in 1986, Rialto Towers was the city's tallest building. The Southbank Promenade, with easy access to restaurants and entertainment venues, was developed in the 1980s and 1990s. Melbourne hosted its first Australian Grand Prix at Melbourne Grand Prix Circuit in 1996. The Crown Melbourne, the city's first gambling centre, was opened in Melbourne. In 2003, the city experienced a huge thunderstorm which resulted in much physical damage. Thunderstorms on a similar scale recurred in 2005 and 2010. "Black Saturday", when the city experienced one of its worst bushfires, took place in 2009. The city celebrated its 175th birthday in 2010.

GOVERNMENT
Australia is both a representative democracy and a constitutional monarchy with Queen Elizabeth II as Australia's head of state. Power is shared between three levels of government: federal, state and local.

The Federal Parliament exercises exclusive powers under the Australian Constitution on issues such as defence, trade, foreign affairs, immigration, copyright, marriage and divorce. The Victorian state government is responsible for law and order, schools, hospitals, water, transport, agriculture and forests. Some powers are shared between the Federal and State Parliaments in areas such as roads, environmental management and public health. If there is conflict in the laws, the federal law takes precedence.

The Constitution defines the powers and responsibilities of the Parliament of Victoria. It specifies that the Parliament of Victoria comprises the Crown, a Legislative Council and a Legislative Assembly. The Government of Victoria follows the Westminster system of government, modelled on the British system.

The three main arms are the executive, legislature and judiciary. In Victoria, the executive power rests formally with the Executive Council, which consists of the Governor and senior ministers. In practice however it is the Premier of Victoria who exercises executive power. Such appointment is based on having a majority support of members of the Legislative Assembly. The premier sets up the Cabinet to run the state government. The Victorian Parliament exercises legislative power. It comprises Elizabeth II, Queen of Australia, who is represented by the Governor of Victoria, and the two Houses, the Victorian Legislative Council (the upper house) and the Victorian Legislative Assembly (the lower house). The Supreme Court of Victoria and the system of subordinate courts exercise judicial power.

Victoria's State Government

Victoria came under the administration of New South Wales and was known as the Port Phillip District of New South Wales. In 1851, Victoria became independent and gained self-government in 1855. The first parliament met in 1856 and made three significant contributions: the drafting of a Constitution, a secret ballot for parliamentary elections, and the building of Parliament House on Spring Street.

Parliament has fixed four year terms. Generally, there

is a general election every four years and members of the Legislative Council and Legislative Assembly stand for election. Voting is compulsory for every Australian citizen aged 18 years and above. Women were entitled to vote in Victoria in 1908 (indigenous women in 1923) and could stand for a seat in Parliament in 1923.

Among the major parties are the Australian Labor Party (ALP), which holds the largest number of seats in the Legislative Assembly and therefore forms the Government. The Liberal Party of Australia and the National Party of Australia are in coalition to form the Opposition, with the largest number of seats in the Assembly outside of the Government. The Australian Greens secured its first seats in the Legislative Council in 2006, and gained seats in both the Assembly and the Council in 2014. But given the changeable nature of politics, winds of change may blow again with the Victorian state elections in 2018 and the Australian federal election the year after that.

ECONOMY

Melbourne is located in the state of Victoria which represents 3 per cent of Australia's total land mass. Victoria has a triple A credit rating from Standard & Poor's and Moody's, reflecting a strong economic performance and good financial management. Victoria has a diverse economy: It is the country's largest supplier of premium food and fibre products, with international education being Victoria's largest service-based export and its aerospace industry a key supplier to the global aviation supply chain. The state accounts for 24 per cent of the national GDP.

The City of Melbourne accounts for 25 per cent of Victoria's Gross State Product and 6 per cent of the national GDP. The city's economy is larger than Singapore's, Hong Kong's and New Zealand's. The City of Melbourne's Census of Land

and Employment (CLUE) reports Melbourne's status as a knowledge city, with more than a quarter of the new jobs in the past ten years created in professional, scientific and technical services. According to their website, such workers want to live where they work, don't necessarily want a car and they are happy to walk, cycle or use public transport. This profile differs from the average Australian. IBM, BP, Siemens are among the world's top companies which are located in Melbourne.

CHAPTER 3

PEOPLE

MELBOURNATION
T SHIRTS

> ❛Twenty years ago it was the cultural elites who used to cringe at the stereotypical Paul Hogan, Steve Irwin and Shane Warne view of Australia. Now that's part of a much broader discussion. People are very aware of what the world imagines Australia to be, and what we really are.❜

— Dr Rebecca Huntley, Ipsos Mackay Research

This is a true story. A relative of mine who migrated from Malaysia to Melbourne some 30 years ago wanted to prepare her children for their new life. She took them to see *Crocodile Dundee,* the movie where Paul Hogan was the quintessential Australian living in the outback. The reality of Melbourne was quite different in the 1980s to that depicted in the movie and today both she and her children laugh about this.

Who is a typical Australian? Certainly not Paul Hogan with his macho ways and an Akubra hat wrestling with the wildlife in the bush or Hugh Jackman with his macho image and rippling muscles as the drover in the Hollywood blockbuster, *Australia.* According to a BBC report in 2013, the quintessential Australian is not a rugged male or a blonde in a bikini but a married thirty-seven year old woman who has two children and lives in a suburban Australian city in a three-bedroom house.

Professor Donald Horne is his seminal work, *The Lucky Country,* described Australia as the world's first suburban nation, and Australians as largely suburban creatures who love their homes and gardens. In Melbourne which is situated in Victoria (both a garden state and the education state), suburban lives still revolve around the home and garden and there is an increased openness to tolerance. So what endears today's society to the average Australian?

For me, the Australian "no worries" attitude and sense of mateship, both of which have been superficially embraced by the world.

There are people from more than 200 nationalities living in Melbourne. Among the diverse ethnicities are peoples from Britain, China, Greece, India, Italy, New Zealand and Vietnam. Over the years this has created a unique Melburnian milieu which has embraced this multicultural ragout based on a generally open and tolerant society. However as a foreigner or newcomer to Melbourne, while most of your experiences may be positive, you might experience some rudeness or hostility as the city evolves to accept the onslaught of new migrants with different tongues and manners.

A disenchanted migrant once remarked that Melbourne is overrated and boring. According to him, it offers a middle class life in the suburbs where most people talk about the weather. As a city dweller who is used to the fast pace of life

and living in the midst of an open economy where you are only too aware of the geopolitical challenges around us, living in Melbourne has brought a sense of freedom and peace. You can find your own space here and your own meaning without having to run the rat race. Whether you wish to be an average Joe or aspire for more, this city lets you decide.

As D.H. Lawrence wrote, "You feel free in Australia. There is great relief in the atmosphere – a relief from tension, from pressure, an absence of control of will or form. The skies open above you and the areas open around you."

STEREOTYPES AND REALITY

Australians are known for being frank and blunt. They will call a spade a spade and their insensitivity may cause offense. To the European, Australians appear loud and crude, lacking polish and refinement. To the Asian the Australian's frankness may be construed as rudeness. To the British, their Aussie cousins are un-English, with lower class cockney accents, rough and lack the formality and pomposity of the British. There is also the stereotype as the Aussie being lazy, a dole bludger and a racist, which is based on their perceptions from home media reports. Australians tend to be informal in speech and their love of informality has raised more than a few eyebrows. There is an oft-cited story of how cricketer Dennis Lillee met Queen Elizabeth at Buckingham Palace in 1981 to receive his Most Excellent Order of the British Empire (MBE). He raised his hands for a handshake and said, "G'day, how ya goin'?"

OPENNESS

Australia has welcomed people into the country since the Second World War. The White Australia policy which existed until 1945 reversed as a result of the country's growing economic needs as foreign labour and talent was used to fill the job vacancies. The post war mood called for greater unity, understanding and connection between ethnic and linguistic groups as many Italians, Greeks and other Europeans came to live in Melbourne, some assisted by government funding. Asian immigration since the 1980s and more recently Muslim and African immigration have met with some resistance and resentment. The indigenous people too have not viewed immigrants too favourably as they feel misplaced and their place as the first people of the nation has taken much time to receive its due recognition after years of discrimination and abuse. The media stereotype of them as social misfits does not help.

However Melbourne in recent years has been more welcoming of new faces, people, and tongues. The city is increasingly known as an open society and many favour multiculturalism with its diverse contribution to society and the economy. Some migrants have taken on anglicised names in an effort to fit in with mainstream society while others have done so to avoid the mispronunciation of their ethnic names. In terms of foods that are available, there is everything from sushi to pasta to dosas and dim sums. Life is more exciting with these diverse offerings.

The increasing number of migrants have led to pressures within the society. A study by the Australia Bureau of Statistics showed that Melbourne has topped the list with a 2.7 per cent increase in population growth in 2018. There is a perceived threat to jobs and Aussie culture by some as many migrants settle in Melbourne. It will take time to develop a meaningful conversation between native Melburnians and new migrants.

MATESHIP

The Australian concept of mateship is a value that is recognised globally. What is the history behind this?

As early as 1885, an Englishman William Lane equated the ideology of socialism with the desire to be mates. He lived briefly in Brisbane before he moved to Paraguay to set up a utopian colony known as New Australia.

Mateship describes the bonds of loyalty and equality, feelings of solidarity and fraternity that Australians exhibit. In 2001, Bendigo Bank ran an advertisement offering mate rates on personal loans.

The usual definition given to the term "mate" is a ubiquitous form of address indicating friendliness and equality. The Lingo Dictionary of Favorite Australian Words and Phrases states that the term "mate" is used to greet someone whose name you can't remember while it has even been suggested that mateship contains a suggestion of corruption.

Throughout the 1990s, then Prime Minister John Howard regarded mateship as a quintessentially Australian value, describing it as a hallowed Australian word that meant more than the relations between people. In September 2006, John Howard's government included mateship as a part of a prospective Australian citizenship test that involved demonstrating an understanding and commitment to Australia and our way of life. To pass, you would need to correctly answer 12 out of 20 questions in the test. While some saw this as an attempt to weed out non-Australian elements and smacked of racism, the bill became law on 12 September 2007.

Mateship has been promoted as a theme in Australian novels and media productions. Tim Winton's *Breath,* now a movie starring Simon Baker, explores the theme of mateship with surfing and sexual danger. In 2006, then Prime Minister Kevin Rudd restated the Australian value of mateship when he said "Mateship is about having a care and concern about someone other than yourself". Julia Gillard, who replaced Rudd as Prime Minister, sought to unite the country on Australia Day in 2011: "More than anything else, Australians are defined by mateship … and the whole world has marvelled at that spirit of mateship in Australia … that is what Australians do …" This rousing reference to mateship came as the country met with environmental challenges such as floods and cyclones.

Undoubtedly the Australian value of mateship exists today. It may have been used to political and economic advantage over the years, but it still runs deep as a value which unites Australians. In his book *Mateship – A Very Australian History*, Nick Dyrenfurth says that "mateship remains a personal and national ideal worth of our aspirations." Former Prime Minister Malcolm Turnbull introduced the term "mateship" to Americans when he visited Washington in early 2018. He described the two countries as "mates" united by the shared values of democracy and rule of law.

"Mateship is reserved for those who share an unspoken bond of friendship, trust, commitment and shared values. Mates stick by each other through good times and bad. Mates have each other's backs," Mr Turnbull wrote. "That is the relationship Australians share with Americans."

Australians place a high value on friendships. In Asia and much of the developed world, there is a silent competition among your neighbours and living up to the Joneses is common. In Australia, there is a sense of fair play and a belief that everyone should "have a fair go", meaning everyone makes mistakes and everyone deserves a break.

VALUES

The Department of Home Affairs has a statement of Australian values which certain visa applicants, including aspiring citizens, must read, agree and sign to. The changes to the Australian citizenship test in June 2017 were aimed at protecting and promoting these values. What exactly are they? According to then Prime Minister Malcolm Turnbull, "there is something uniquely Australian about them".

Among the values stated are that "respect for the freedom and dignity of the individual, freedom of religion, commitment to the rule of law, Parliamentary democracy, equality of men and women and a spirit of egalitarianism that embraces mutual respect, tolerance, fair play and compassion for those in need and pursuit of the public good; Australian society values equality of opportunity for individuals, regardless of their race, religion or ethnic background; and that the English language, as the national language, is an important unifying element of Australian society."

Recent data about the percentage of Australians who speak English at home is decreasing. It may be hard to realise the Australian dream of spoken English being the unifying element of Australian society.

In an ABC interview on the 2017 Lowry Institute poll on how Australians view the world and the country's direction, it appears that up to half the Australians polled are divided about the country's direction (48 per cent dissatisfied) and a majority of Australians (79 per cent) are dissatisfied with the world's direction. Yet they believe that globalisation is "mostly good" for Australia, and most believe in the benefits of free trade (78 per cent) .

New Zealand is seen as a country that Australia can trust, followed by the United States. China is viewed both as a potential military threat in the future but an important economic partner (79 per cent). The perceived interference by the Chinese in Australian politics surfaced in late 2017 when Labour Senator Sam Dastyari resigned as senator when it was revealed that he had received massive donations from Beijing-linked millionaire Huang Xiangmao.

Although parliamentary democracy is identified as an Australian value, this poll has found that only 60 per cent (and an even smaller percentage of younger Australians) believe that democracy is the best form of government.

ABC News (Australian Broadcasting Corporation, a national news service) published a list of quintessentially Australian values, and I attempt to explain them below:

Nature Strip

It is true that Australians treasure the nature strips in front of their houses. Although council regulations usually state that the nature strip in front of your home is shared land, most Australians use this space to dump their garbage whether it is furniture or appliances outside of hard rubbish day (the official days for getting rid of hard furniture) This allows a passer-by to take a look and decide whether this is something they need.

Taxi Rides and Authority

In Australia, when you ride a taxi, you sit in the front seat and not the back. This is because Australian society is based on egalitarian principles and everyone is a mate so you would sit with the driver. Given their convict background, Australians are said to be anti-authority. The reality is that there is a plethora of local government and there are penalties for breaking laws.

Sausage Sizzles

A common sight in the weekend are sausage sizzles outside Bunnings for the purpose of fund raising. During elections too, there are sausage sizzles at polling places humorously referred to as democracy sausages.

Sports Mania

The national obsession is sports and if you want to fit in, you need to know about the sport in Melbourne whether it is rugby, cricket or tennis.

A Love of TV

The Gold Logie award given for the entertainment industry is based on popular vote. The Most Popular Personality is awarded by the public. This is as close to any Australian interest in democracy or politics as Australians are generally apolitical.

Days Off Work

Australians do not need a reason to take a day off. From events such as the Queen's birthday to horse racing and Footy, Melburnians have taken a day off to celebrate.

Sausage sizzles outside Bunnings

Larrikins

Australian use the term "larrikins" when they refer to themselves. Larrikins are people with a disregard for convention; a tradition that idolises mischief and finds humour in life.

Australians love talking about what it means to be Australian, and people in Melbourne are no different, with many television talk shows discussing the issue. Many Australians like the idea that they are seen as laid back and non-mainstream. Swearing too is part of the culture. However, in Melbourne, depending on who you speak to and interact with, you may find that many ethnic groups retain their cultural practices and still proudly call themselves Australian. In fact it may be common for a Croatian who has lived in Australia for several years to refer to themselves as a Croatian Australian. Being at the bottom end of the world, Australians have lived with the knowledge that their geographical location leaves them isolated from the rest of the world. What was initially a huge problem for the early settlers, due to the tyranny of distance, has become a strength as many tourists, visitors and would-be migrants visit Melbourne to enjoy the largely unspoilt landscape and high living standards. The physical isolation gives a sense of being far away from the madding crowd.

Sense of Community

Hugh Mackay, an Australian social researcher and Honorary Professor of Social Science at the University of Wollongong has raised awareness of a "loss of community" in neighbourhoods as a concern among contemporary Australians. This may be compounded by language barriers as new neighbours may not be as conversant in English. "We don't know our neighbours" has become a cliché of contemporary urban life.

GOING GREEN

Australians are concerned with the environment and recycling is practised in Melbourne. The weekly kerbside garbage is divided into three bins, one for general waste, one for paper and recycled products and a green bin for grass, flowers and garden waste. In general about 51 per cent of household waste gets recycled in Australia which is consistent with recycling rates in northern European countries. Since 30 June 2018, major supermarkets like Coles and Woolworths do not provide plastic bags to shoppers. Instead shoppers are encouraged to bring their own green bag. Both supermarkets offered rewards to customers who brought their own bags in the initial period. Recyclable or reusable plastic bags can be purchased.

TRADITIONS

Australia shares most of the English traditions such as Easter, Christmas and the New Year. However, celebrating these traditions Down Under brings a new twist in the heat.

Christmas is celebrated in summer and is a family celebration of seafood and pavlovas. You can always roast

the traditional turkey but given the heat, most Australians would have a barbecue instead. The barbecue could range from a simple spread of meats roasted on a barbecue to more extravagant seafood with prawns and lobsters on the grill. Desserts, apart from the traditional Christmas pudding, have a more seasonal flavour with a platter of fresh mangoes and cherries.

Easter is celebrated more as a secular event in Melbourne although there are religious activities and services surrounding Easter in churches around the city. Melburnians rush to buy their stock of Easter chocolates and the tempting varieties by Lindt, Cadbury and Ferrero Rocher, are just a few of the sweet offerings you can enjoy. The traditional hot cross buns have morphed into apple cinnamon, chocolate, chocolate chips and other varieties to satisfy the gourmet.

The New Year is usually ushered in with house parties, dinner parties, dining at restaurants, and counting down to the New Year with fireworks at the city centre.

Anzac Day

The Australian and New Zealand Army Corps (Anzac) Day celebrated on 25 April is in honour of Australians who have died in wars. It is highly celebrated with dawn services, city marches by veterans and drinks in the afternoon. The services are held at war memorials throughout Australia and are sober events with hymns, laying of wreaths, a period of silence, and the National Anthem.

Traditionally Anzac day was an event to remember the Australians who had fought in the First World War, and the losses at Gallipoli. Today it is to remember the soldiers who have fought in more recent wars including Afghanistan.

In *The One Day of the Year*, a play by Alan Seymour about a father and son at war over the commemoration of the landing at Gallipoli and focused on the changing attitudes of the young, there is a scene when the son shouts, "It's just about one long grog-up. We're sick of all the muck that's talked about this day… Every year you still march down that street with that stupid, proud expression on your face, you glorify the wastefulness of that day."

His father hits back, "You'd take away everything, You'd take away the ordinary bloke's right to feel a bit proud of himself for once."

Those powerful words remain true today as Anzac Day still attracts many to the dawn ceremonies and other events remembering those who have fought in wars from Australia.

Australia Day

Australia Day on 26 January commemorates the founding of Australia in 1788 when the first British fleet arrived at Port Jackson, New South Wales and the Governor Arthur Philip raised the flag of Great Britain at Sydney Cove. In recent years this celebration has been marred by critiques of the British invasion of Australia and abuse of the local Aborigines. However, despite this controversy, the day is celebrated with parties, picnics, and fireworks and community and family events. On Australia Day, countless listeners tune to the Triple J Hottest 100 to find out which song has been voted number one.

Boxing Day

The day after Christmas is another excuse to party or continue shopping as there are massive Boxing Day sales in Melbourne. Chadstone Shopping Centre is especially busy as the sales attract not only local Melbournians but international visitors. Boxing Day is comparable to America's Black Friday. For those who are not keen on shopping, there is cricket. Cricket fans would be busy and spend the day after Christmas on the couch, stubby in hand, air-con turned up high, watching and soon after falling asleep in front of the Boxing Day Test Cricket.

AFL Grand Final

The AFL Grand Final holiday is the newest public holiday in the state of Victoria. The Friday before the Australian Football League Grand Final is a public holiday and is referred to as "AFL Grand Final Friday". Despite the economic costs, it is an event that is celebrated by most Australians who are fanatical about footy.

There are 18 teams competing in the league. Before the Final series, there will be 23 rounds and there are 27 pre-season practice matches played over February and March. Watching the Grand Final Day, whether at home from your television or in person at the Melbourne Cricket Ground (MCG) is the culmination of the sports fever experienced throughout the year. The atmosphere will be electrifying and passionate supporters will be seen and heard during the game.

Schoolies

A tradition since the 1970s, this is when final year students, usually Year 12 students, celebrate their freedom by going on a school holiday (sans teachers and parents) to a beach, usually the Gold Coast, for a weeklong party of alcohol and fun.

Carols by Candlelight

Carols by Candlelight has been an Australian family tradition in Melbourne since 1938. The event, which is celebrated on the night of Christmas Eve, is held at the Sidney Myer Bowl where family and friends enjoy live performances and join in the singing of Christmas carols. It was made popular by radio announcer Norman Banks in 1937 and both locals and tourists gather on Christmas eve. It is a ticketed event.

Myer's Christmas Windows

Myer's Christmas Windows has been an annual event since 1956. This tradition is enjoyed by Melburnians and attracts more than a million visitors each year. The windows traditionally display Christmas stories such as *The Twelve Days of Christmas*, *How the Grinch Stole Christmas*, *A Christmas Carol*, *How Santa Really Works*, *Peter Pan*, *Sleeping Beauty,* and *Snow White and the Seven Dwarfs*. Entry to the windows is free.

REFUGEE POLICY

Australia's asylum seeking policy demands that those who reach Australia by boat must be sent to an offshore processing centre while their claims are being processed. Nauru in the Pacific and Manus Island in Papua New Guinea are two such centres. There has been much criticism both for and against these centres and the treatment of these asylum seekers in terms of facilities provided. Even if they are found to be genuine asylum seekers, the policy now requires that such people settle in Nauru or Papua New Guinea. An opinion poll released by Roy Morgan in 2017 found Australians to be evenly divided on whether refugees at off-shore centres should be allowed to enter the country. However the UN and Amnesty International have condemned the off-shore processing system as cruel and inhumane, causing widespread despair, self-harm and suicide attempts among those affected. A Melbourne-based lawyer Julian Burnside successfully appealed to a Federal court to allow a suicidal ten-year-old child on Nauru to come to Australia for psychiatric treatment.

In 2015, the government announced that a total of 12,000 additional Humanitarian Program places would be made available to Syrians and Iraqis affected by the war. This yearly intake has been increasing and will rise to 18,750 places from 2018-19. There are community hubs to help refugees access government and other services within their local community. These hubs provide a range of services from playgroups for pre-school children with multi-lingual storytelling, English classes, sewing groups and coffee circles. Trained staff and volunteers provide support, advice and mentoring.

When it was first reported in 2016 that a block of about 60 unused units on the same site as the St Vincent's aged care facility in Eltham would be used as a resettlement site, there were protests by far-right groups in the Battle for Eltham. Locals in Eltham rallied together in support of the refugees, and since December 2016, Eltham has welcomed Iranian and Syrian refugees with warmth and hospitality, providing household essentials and a welcome book signed by hundreds of locals. They have even organised English lessons and subsidised driving lessons.

ABORIGINES

Australia has admitted to its mistreatment of the native Australians, the Aborigines. In his book *The Secret Country*, John Pilger, an Australian award winning journalist and documentary maker, postulated that Aborigines had been in the past considered as part of the fauna and not considered as human. Today there is recognition of this abuse and in 2008, former Prime Minister Kevin Rudd was the first Prime Minister to publicly acknowledge and apologise to the Stolen Generation: Aboriginal children who were forcibly taken away from their families to resettle and assimilate with white Anglo Saxon families were the Stolen Generation.

There is an apparent respect for the Aborigines as each council in Melbourne acknowledges the original people who live in the land. For example, the Aborigines who lived in Melbourne city were the Kulin peoples. In everyday life however, it is rare to socialise and meet Aborigines. They are more in country Victoria than in the cities. A Kiwi friend commented that unlike New Zealand where you would see Maoris in the city, in Melbourne, you hardly see many

Aborigines in Melbourne. While Aboriginal culture has many traditions, they do not appear to be a part of public life with the exception of Moomba. Theirs is a tragic tale of total annihilation and destruction due to the white settlers in Melbourne. According to Dr Clare Land, a historian with Monash University, "the 15 years leading up to the gold rush was an incredibly rapid and brutal colonisation in which a lot of Aboriginal people were gotten rid of."

Tunnerminnerwait and Maulboyheener

There is the tale of two young Aboriginals, Tunnerminnerwait and Maulboyheener from Tasmania who fled to Melbourne in 1839 to avoid being killed. Unfortunately, they found that the same predicament would await them in Melbourne. They tried to escape and got into a fight with white settlers where the latter were killed in self defence. Eventually both Tunnerminnerwait and Maulboyheener were tried and sentenced to execution in 1842, in an unfair process where they were not allowed to give evidence as they were not Christian. Apparently their bodies were taken to the burial site in unmarked graves, (which today is the Queen Victoria Market). Descendants of both Aboriginals have called for a memorial to remember them, and the City of Melbourne council has been under pressure to erect a monument at the execution site on Franklin Street. According to Dr Land, "There is almost no commemoration of frontier conflict in Australia and certainly not in a capital city in Australia."
Source: www.melbourne.vic.gov.au

CHAPTER 4

CUSTOMS

> ❝Ninety-one per cent of Australians are proud to be Australian.❞

— a 2016 poll by the Institute of Public Affairs

Most Australians believe that their country is a great place to live. And going by the rising number of people migrating to Melbourne, you would agree that Melbourne seems to be the place to be for migrants, students, business visitors and tourists.

Having spoken to many newcomers to Melbourne, the general perception is that it is undoubtedly one of the world's friendliest cities. Whether you are asking for directions or a place for coffee or general information, you will find that Melburnians will go out of their way to help you. In fact Melburnians are mostly tolerant and open people and that explains why many migrants are drawn to this city.

A lot of migrants that I have spoken to would point out that the Australians that they have met are of various ethnicities. It was largely a white Australia until the 1970s and then Europeans such as Germans, Dutch, Greek and Maltese and the first Asian refugees, the Vietnamese, followed by the Sri Lankans arrived, and today you get different groups from Asia such as China, India, Singapore and Malaysia who tend to be skilled migrants or business migrants.

It is therefore difficult to stereotype the average Australian. The social mix differs too depending on the suburb. As a generalisation, many Asian Australians reside in Springvale and Footscray. Glen Eira and Toorak is where the rich in Melbourne live. Brunswick is the hipster area with lots of young people, students and professionals. Broadmeadows is largely a Muslim area where many Arabs live.

Asian restaurants

Australians tend to be informal in their language and daily interactions; fellow commuters on public transport will be friendly and pleasant. Anyone who's ever moved to another city knows how difficult it is to make friends, but Melbourne seems to be an exception. Born and bred Melburnians are happy to open up their friendship groups to new people and are generally fairly open-minded. In fact, if you are new to the city, most Melburnians are happy to teach you about their way of life and they will share their time and knowledge to help you settle.

My own experience moving into a residential neighbourhood in a south eastern suburb with a young family in 1998 was positive and my integration into Melbourne was made easier when we became fast friends with an Australian family who had young children in a similar age group as ours. In fact our children got on like a house on fire and they were literally in and out of each other's homes. All my initial trepidation of how the children would settle soon evaporated.

I was also touched by the warmth of the mothers at my

children's school. I was able to slowly build up a conversation with other mothers during play dates. It will take time but you will soon get to know these Aussie mothers and break through their reserve. A Singapore Australian shared her experience that making friends with the school mums at soccer took time as while the parents were polite and friendly at practices and matches, they did not associate beyond their clusters of pre-existing relationships. It took some years before she made real friendships with other mothers.

The culture in Melbourne in 1998 was a bit more English and the mothers had a reserve to them which melted over time and we were able to connect. Some of my earliest impressions of Melbourne were positive because of the warm hospitality that I experienced. Recently, as Melbourne gets more crowded and busy, I see more gesticulations around you, not as friendly faces and some cars honking at traffic lights but thankfully not as much as most frenetic cities.

Australians are very down to earth and do not like people who flaunt their wealth or position. New migrants to Melbourne would be advised not to flaunt their wealth although with the nouveau riche, this advice may fall on deaf ears as they buy up property and drive expensive cars.

FRIENDLINESS—A REALITY?

Hardly anyone I have spoken to would describe Melburnians as other than helpful and friendly. This was my experience in a suburban supermarket, as I walked up and down the aisles looking for jelly crystals to make a dessert. It was a busy period as it was just before Easter and there was quite a crowd. I went to one of the assistants near the bakery and the assistant walked all the way with me to guide me to the correct aisle and shelf to find what I needed. That is excellent service, and an example of how friendly and helpful you will find Melburnians are.

However, digging beneath the surface, a few migrants, both recent and long term, have pointed out that the friendliness may be superficial. Anna, a young European who completed her postgraduate studies in Melbourne and works in the city, found that Australians were very open people, in that they made conversation with strangers and newcomers, but only on a superficial level, as the conversations did not develop into meaningful or intimate conversations.

Henry, an older European friend who migrated to Australia in the 1950s shared that his initial experience was that Melburnians were happy to help him when he first came. However he did suggest that once he established himself and reached the "Australian" standard of living, the tall poppy syndrome surfaced and his Australian friends became less involved in his life.

A young New Zealander who studies and works in Melbourne describes Australians as more outgoing and extroverted compared to Kiwis. Most often this is positive and seen as friendly but sometimes, she is put off by the abrasive or obnoxious Australians.

Another Asian friend, Sam, has pointed out that to really fit into Melbourne culture, you need to know about the culture and the sports. This point was reinforced by another Malaysian friend Cherie who studied in Melbourne and now works here. There is talk about the national sports, footy, at work. It is the custom to Footy Tip every week. You have to know which teams played over the weekend and which won.

Having observed the interactions of many friends and family, it is noteworthy that older people tend to socialise with not only their racial groups but rather social groups such as parent groups, colleagues, by age, by club, by interests, by work. Young people however have assimilated a lot more at school and there are genuine friendships made across different ethnic groups.

If you want to fit into Melbourne society, find a social group that you can enjoy and you will find it easier to settle in. You will feel more connected to the community if you are involved in more groups that interest you.

> *Floating Life*, a 1996 movie directed by Clara Law, is a poignant and funny film about a Chinese family that falls apart after moving from Hong Kong to Australia. It explores the new migrant experience of a family from Hong Kong as they adjust to life in an Australian suburb. Among the challenges faced by the family are the dogs in the street and the vast open spaces. The heavy sense of displacement felt by one of the children results in a nervous breakdown. The whole family's experience evolves from excitement to fear before there is adjustment and acceptance.

CRIME GANGS

In the annual survey of social cohesion conducted by Andrew Markus of Monash University for the Scanlon Foundation, it was found that six million Australians hold very or somewhat negative views of Muslims.

The Sudanese problem of crime gangs in Melbourne do not help temper negative views about the latest migrants to the city. In 2011, footballer Nelly Yoa, a Sudanese migrant to Melbourne, was a victim of a high-profile machete attack. Data from Victoria's Crime Statistics Agency shows an overrepresentation in some crime categories of Sudanese-born and Kenyan-born offenders in proportion to their Victorian populations.

However, some social commentators have pointed out that over time, this has been a moving target. Australians have changed the target of their fear from the Italian mafia, to unemployed youth gangs (white boys) terrorising suburbs, to Vietnamese, Lebanese and Middle Eastern gangs, and most recently the Sudanese gangs.

A MULTICULTURAL SOCIETY

A 2015 survey by the Scanlon Foundation showed that while Australia still views itself as an immigrant nation, where 86 per cent of respondents agreed that "multiculturalism has been good for Australia", only a minority felt that there should be support for ethnic minorities to retain their customs and traditions. Most of the support is from young adults who grew up in a diverse cultural environment and are digital natives.

A University of Melbourne migrant youth survey in 2018 revealed that while a majority—82 per cent—of respondents (refugee and migrants youth aged between 15 to 25) feel optimistic about their futures, there are feelings of discrimination and fears for their safety. The survey gathered the views of nearly 200 young people from September and October 2017. It claims to be the first and most comprehensive national account of how multicultural young people are faring socially, culturally and economically. Those surveyed opined that diversity and discrimination were the most important issues facing Australia.

SOCIAL CUSTOMS

The most noticeable difference between Australians and newcomers is in the way we approach food and eating. Asians are casual and generous with food and any invitation to a meal in a friend's home means an abundance of food, with exhortations to take some extras home. Unlike Asia where every meal is a celebration, lunches in Melbourne tend to be quick and on the go, a maximum of 30 minutes.

Weddings

Melbourne's multicultural mix offers varied and exciting wedding celebrations. An Australian nephew, a Malaysian Tamil who married an Australian Greek, celebrated his wedding with

A row of ethnic restaurants

a modern mix of customs. The civil ceremony was conducted by a Justice of Peace, and incorporated a Greek *stefana*, a circular crown with flower embroideries linked with a ribbon that symbolises the union of two people, and Tamil customs like the tying of a *thali*, a gold chain that the groom ties around the bride's neck. The dancing at the wedding dinner was to pop, Greek and Indian music.

Weddings can be lavish affairs in Melbourne. It is usual to host the wedding at a reception hall or a hotel depending on your budget. For the Australian-Sri Lankan Christian community whose customs I am familiar with, the guest list can range in the hundreds. There is a church wedding for Christians followed by a reception of a dinner and dance. There will be time for speeches during the course of the wedding and for the couple usually begins the dance segment with the first dance.

A friend, Mary, who attended an Italian wedding at St Patrick's Cathedral in the 1990s, recalled how lavish the celebrations were, with 400 guests, a bridal party of a dozen people, and a five-tiered cake. It was a huge celebration.

Pearl, a Hong Kong Australian who has lived in Melbourne for 30 years has attended many weddings involving young

Australians of Hong Kong descent. Similar to the Chinese style weddings she was used to back home, the general practice is a Chinese-style banquet dinner for close friends and immediate family while an afternoon tea at church would involve a wider group of work colleagues and acquaintances.

Some young couples who get married today tend to be more casual and informal about their celebration. The venue may range from the parents' home or garden, a wedding reception venue, a restaurant or a vineyard.

Funerals

Attending a wake or funeral service is a formal affair. They are regarded as private matters. You cannot decide to attend a wake without an invitation. A family member of the deceased would have to inform you of the details of the service. This is unlike Asia where funeral details are published in the newspaper and most people attend funerals of loved ones out of respect, with or without an invitation. However, in Melbourne you would not be advised to do so.

Baby's First Birthday

Depending on the family, a baby's first birthday may be a small affair or a big party. Some Australians do celebrate the baby's first birthday with a big bang choosing venues such as a restaurant, play area or at home with hired props like trampolines. For toddlers to teens, other party venues include the zoo, theme venues and even art galleries. Asia cultures too tend to celebrate this milestone. Some traditional cultures like the Europeans in Melbourne may not have a big party but a close family celebration.

18th and 21st Birthday Celebrations

The 18th birthday party celebration ranks alongside the 21st birthday celebration as a mega celebration for young people in Melbourne. Very often it is organised by parents who go the extra mile to fulfil their child's coming of age in an extravagant celebration. Naturally a lot would depend on the socio-economic background of the parents. Planning the birthday would involve detailed planning. Choosing the venue is based on your budget and such a milestone celebration may be held at home, at a hired hall, in a high end club or restaurant or a pub. Safety is a consideration at such parties as Australians are known for their love of alcohol and a group of 18-year-olds would require supervision.

You would also be advised to inform your neighbours about the party if you're having it at home as the noise level could be extremely high. You would also need to check with the local council on noise restrictions after midnight and avoid angering your neighbours. Setting house rules is also a must and locking up your valuables would be prudent. Informing the local police in advance may help as they may monitor the area. As public transport may not be an option after midnight, it would be good to advise your child to inform the parents to pick up the children after the party or arrange for them to sleep over.

The 21st birthday party is similar with the same issues in terms of budget, venue and theme. Safety and the serving of alcohol (and not drugs) is something to take note of. If you are from a conservative background, you may not wish to serve alcohol in your party. Melburnians are used to bringing their own alcohol to the venue.

Short speeches are common at a 21st birthday party and it is customary that one of the parents speaks about the child's achievements and what makes them special as they begin their journey in adulthood.

Public Displays of Affection
At work, it is advisable not to greet co-workers with a kiss on

the cheek as it may be misinterpreted. The Me Too movement has raised awareness to the problem of male superiors taking advantage of female subordinates at the workplace. However if you are socialising at a restaurant, a greeting on the cheek is acceptable.

Public displays of affection by couples confined to hand holding is acceptable in most countries and definitely in Melbourne. Passionate displays between a couple even in liberal Melbourne are generally not seen. So drunken couples in awkward displays such as a passionate kiss would be frowned upon.

SPORTING EVENTS

When I attended the Australian Open, I was impressed by the relaxed efficiency with which the event was conducted. There were no loud, bold signs on where to queue and yet most people were happy to queue without jostling and entry into the Olympic Park was smooth. Getting into the various courts—Margaret Court, Rod Laver Arena, Hisense Court— with the right pass was easy and you could walk around throughout the day and buy food and drinks inside. The event attracts international visitors and locals, and is family friendly although the night session sees a lot more drink and party. The atmosphere is carnival-like and there are attractions such as a theme park and face painting for children.

Serene, a Asian Australian, had her first taste of an Australian sporting event at a footy game where the mood was electric. She explained the appeal of the game as Melburnians of different backgrounds, social status and beliefs all congregated and cheered on their respective teams. According to her, footy should be a cultural event as it is truly part of Australian life and culture. Once you watch a footy game, no other contact sporting event comes close.

SOCIAL ETIQUETTE

Driving

Cars are driven on the left hand side of the road. The traffic rules are quite similar to the British rules. If you are new to Melbourne, watch out for the roundabouts and hook turns.

Public Transportation

Whether you are boarding a tram, train or a bus, make sure you wait for existing passengers to leave before you enter. This is a matter of courtesy and shows regard for them.

If you are using the escalator in the train station, you will notice that people stand on the left of the rail and overtake on the right.

Holding the Door

If you use a lift, it is considered courteous to hold the lift doors open for others to enter. Similarly if you are in a public building, and you open the door and there is someone close by, it would be expected that you hold the door open for them, especially if they are trying to rush towards the door.

Queuing

Don't cut the queue in Melbourne. Australians are used to queuing and not cutting the queue. It would be courteous to wait patiently for your turn. If you are in a crowd and in doubt, ask the person next to you whether they are in a queue. Sometimes in a restaurant even after a booking, you would still need to wait your turn as there may be a queue.

Cleanliness

Australians respect their land and try to keep it clean. You will find that in parks, most people carry people carry their rubbish away while in a food court, most people would take their own tray and food scraps to the bin at the food court although there are cleaners around. Despite a lack of enforcement, you would generally find that most Australians do not leave a mess to clean up, in public places. There is no obvious litter or cigarette butts left in parks or picnic sites. In fact, if you have an outdoor barbecue in the public park, you are expected to take away your rubbish. Always be prepared with your own rubbish bags when eating at public places. Sometimes you will find that there are not many rubbish bins.

Treatment of Service Staff

Australians have a strong culture of egalitarianism. No matter the job, treat people with equal respect and use "please", "thank you" and "excuse me" with everyone. Never snap your fingers, whistle or yell at service staff to get their attention. These gestures may be considered rude, and the standard of service you receive may drop as a result of this.

Meal at an Australian Home

What to bring to a dinner: definitely wine. Australians love their wine and many of them are wine connoisseurs. Be warned that Jacob's Creek may be viewed as plonk or cheap wine. Depending upon who is on the guest list, the choice of wine is very important. It would be considered rude if you were to ask about the cost of the wine bottle. It is better to recommend a wine based on its blend and taste. It is acceptable to give a box of chocolates, flowers or a plant as a gift to the host.

Gifts

Small gifts are commonly exchanged with family members, close friends, and neighbours on birthdays and Christmas. Generally, most people go Dutch even on special occasions

such as birthdays. There is no expectation that the host pays for their guests. At the office Kris Kringle or Secret Santa during Christmas time, where everyone buys a small gift for another colleague, the cost is limited to about A$10 per person. Remember that you need to buy a politically correct gift and not something too outlandish. Baby showers for colleagues are also limited to an affordable amount per person such as A$5 per person or as much as you wish. Tradespeople such as construction workers may be given a small amount of cash, and sometimes even a bottle of wine or a six-pack of beer.

Making Small Talk

Aussies are known to be frank but Melburnians tend to be polite and a little reserved. Always use your first name. You would be starting a conversation on the wrong foot if you start talking politics with your neighbour. To be safe, always begin with the weather or sports. Weather is a topic that never goes out of season as the weather in Melbourne can be inclement and changes all the time. Serious topics like religion, politics and sex should be left for your inner circle of friends as you get to know them.

Don't feel like you need to say "G'day, mate" to fit in. Just saying "Hi", "Hello" or "Hello, how are you?" would suffice.

GAY AND LESBIAN SCENE

Melbourne is an open society and LGBTQ people do not congregate in any particular areas. There are gay and lesbian friendly accommodation in Fitzroy, Carlton, St Kilda, South Yarra and Prahran. The Peel located in Fitzroy, is a popular nightclub frequented by the LGBTQ community. Other popular clubs are the Laird and Sircuit.

The Midsumma Festival held from mid-January to early February is an annual festival that includes not only sports, arts and theatre but the Pride March. There is also the Melbourne Queer Film Festival held annually in March since 1991 (mqff.com.au). The ChillOut Festival held in Daylesford Victoria is an annual regional gay pride festival.

A weekly newspaper, the Melbourne Community Voice is a free gay and lesbian paper. Joy 94.9 is a gay and lesbian community radio station.

GLOBE (Gay and Lesbian Organisation of Business and Enterprise) is a not-for-profit community group that welcomes LGBTQ individuals, businesses, community groups and their supporters so they can engage and develop their interests in an environment that encourages diversity and inclusiveness.

The openness to a same-sex lifestyle was proved in the postal referendum in Australia in 2017 where 61 per cent of

Australians voted in favour of same sex marriages. Victoria was the second highest state which voted in favour it. In fact to refer to gays and lesbians as an alternative lifestyle would not be encouraged. Everyone in Melbourne refers to their other half as their partner.

This is a vast contrast to the 1990s when an Australian movie, *Head On* (1998), shocked viewers with its graphic depiction of drugs and a young second generation Greek Australian battling with acceptance of his gay lifestyle.

Same sex marriages have been legalised in Australia since 9 December 2017.

RELIGION

There is an increasing number of Melburnians who profess no religion—about 21 per cent of the population. Many young Australians aged 18-34 fall within this group.

The breakdown of the population in Melbourne according to religious beliefs is similar with national statistics. The predominant religion is Christianity with about 30 per cent Catholic, 12 per cent Anglican, 6 per cent Eastern Orthodox and 4 per cent Uniting Church. Buddhists, Muslims, Jews and Hindus account for 7.5 per cent of the population, an increase over the past decade.

Most people in Melbourne practice freedom of religion and do not openly discuss religious views with one another. The society is secular and many Melburnians do not appreciate the open promotion or confession of faith in public; anyone seen to do so may be met with irritation.

A "Bible ring" has formed in the suburbs surrounding Melbourne Airport and Essendon Airport, where about two thirds of the population are Christian, as well as in the eastern suburbs, although the number of Christians is not as significant.

The inner-city suburbs of Brunswick, Northcote, St Kilda and Richmond are where those who profess "no religion" are the majority. Islam has been identified as the main religion in Dallas, Broadmeadows and Meadow Heights while Jews predominantly reside in Caulfield and Buddhists in Springvale South.

CHAPTER 5

SETTLING IN

> ❝Their cities are safe and clean and nearly always built on water. They have a society that is prosperous, well ordered, and instinctively egalitarian. The food is excellent. The beer is cold. The sun nearly always shines. There is coffee on every corner. Life doesn't get much better than this.❞

— **Bill Bryson, *In a Sunburned Country***

Several categories of visas are available to individuals qualified to work or train in an eligible skilled occupation in Australia. The list of occupations is reviewed by the Department of Jobs and Small Businesses regularly. A current list can be found on the Department of Home Affairs website, https://immi.homeaffairs.gov.au. An applicant can find a sponsor or put in an expression of interest.

For those who wish to apply for permanent residence, there are several options: the family-stream permanent residence visa, work-stream permanent residence visa and the business or investment-stream permanent residence visa. Details of these visas can be found at https://immi.homeaffairs.gov.au/visas/permanent-resident/visa-options.

There is also a retirement visa pathway available for eligible retirees: long-term residents who have contributed to, and are well established in the community.

STUDY VISA

To qualify you must have been accepted to study full-time at an educational institution in Australia and secured an organised welfare arrangement for your stay if you are under 18 years of age.

You must be enrolled in a course of study that is registered on the Commonwealth Register of Institutions and courses for

Overseas Students (CRICOS), and receive confirmation before you enter Australia. The usual requirements are evidence of English language proficiency and financial capacity that covers course fees, travel and living costs. Other requirements are passing the health test, having health insurance and meeting the character requirements. Primary or secondary school students may also apply for a visa to study in Australia.

This visa allows you to stay in Australia for the duration of your studies, generally up to five years.

Skilled Migration Program – An Alternative View

In a report by the Australian Population Research Institute in March 2018 entitled *Australia's Skilled Migration Program: Scarce Skills Not Required,* Bob Birrell posited that the government's migration programme was motivated by financial, business and property interests rather than a need for scarce skills.

According to the report, the government's argument that "any major cut to the migration programme would put in jeopardy Australia's 26 years of unbroken nominal economic growth" was misplaced. Drawing on the unpublished data on occupations in the skills programme, it reported that those obtaining visas faced difficulties obtaining a job as professionals due to an oversupply. What the economy needed were skilled construction workers. The Skills Occupation List (SOL), introduced in 2010, aimed at selecting occupations based on the national shortage, had been abolished in 2016. The Medium to Long-Term Strategic Skill List (MLTSSL), which replaces it, selects occupations based on a two- to ten-year forecast, not on present demand.

According to Birrell, this has resulted in unemployment for new migrants seeking to find professional work. The 2016 census indicates that only 24 per cent of migrants from non–English speaking countries (aged between 25 and 34) were employed as professionals, compared with 50 per cent of migrants from English-speaking countries and 58 per cent of same aged Australian-born graduates. This is compounded by the increasing number of domestic graduates who are competing for jobs in the market. The 2017 Report on Graduate Outcomes had revealed that only 53.5 per cent of domestic undergraduates were able to obtain employment upon graduation as of April 2017.

Source: The Australian Population Research Institute, Research Report, March 2018, found at tapri.org.au.

FINDING A HOME

There are several websites to find a place to rent or buy: www.realestate.com.au, www.rent.com.au and www.domain.com.au.

Most migrants find it relatively easier to rent than buy. If you are new to Melbourne and you have no credit history, you may need to provide evidence of creditworthiness from overseas to rent a home. The process takes time and the availability of homes in desired suburbs is competitive.

Buying a house takes some planning and quite some money. The housing prices in Melbourne has escalated with growing demand from locals, migrants and foreign investors. Inner city prices can be in the millions while the outer suburbs are more affordable.

Furnishing

From new to second hand, buying furniture is easy in Melbourne. There are high-end furniture shops such as Domayne, Great Dane, Living Edge, Jardan, and more on Chapel Street and in Richmond; mid-range shops like IKEA, Early Settler, Freedom, discount furniture at Fantastic Furniture and second hand furniture available on www.gumtree.com.au. You can find streets of furniture hubs to stroll through in various suburbs such as St Kilda, Nunawading, Dandenong and the Western suburbs.

You can search online for furniture at various websites: www.homestyleoutlet.com.au, www.zilloandhutch.com, www.informationvine.com, www.makemypiece.com.au and www.myshopping.com.au.

Appliances

For appliances, the stores to visit are Harvey Norman, Good Guys, JB Hi-Fi and Cosco. These stores also have an online presence.

Moving

Crown, Removalist Australia, www.johnryan.com.au; melbournecheapremovalists.com.au; www.transaus melbourne.com.au; movefinders.com.au; Word of mouth; www.oneflare.com.au

Books

In 2008, Melbourne was named by UNESCO as Australia's first and only City of Literature. You will find independent players such as The Paperback Bookshop, Readings, Hill of Content (Melbourne's oldest bookstore), Avenue Bookstore, The Grumpy Swimmer and Eltham Bookshop. Specialty bookstores include Embiggen Books (art, design, photography, architecture), Perimeter Books (small press titles, books and zines), The Little Book Room (children's) and Books for Cooks (cookbooks). Of course, there are also secondhand bookstores and the retail chains like Dymocks. Worth special mentions are Buck Mulligan's (whisky

A branch of independent book retailer Readings

bar-cum-bookstore that stocks only Irish writers) and Willows & Wine (wine bar-cum-secondhand bookstore).

WHAT TO BRING FROM HOME

Settling into new surroundings is made easier when you have what is familiar to you. The first time I came to Melbourne as a student, I came with my family and two young children who were in kindergarten and primary school. Having the same beds to sleep in, with their favourites stuffed animals and toys helped them feel more at home.

The mistake we made was bringing our electrical appliances. The second time around, I did not make the same mistake as appliances are affordable in Melbourne and there a host of retailers which offer a range of products from high-end Miele to midrange Samsung appliances. You would not need to spend unnecessary time rewiring these appliances with suitable power plugs. The electrical plug used in Melbourne is a 10 amp Type 1 similar to New Zealand, Papua New Guinea, China and Argentina.

Buying a new wardrobe for every member of the family would be expensive. Bearing in mind the often changeable Melbourne weather, it is best to pack for both summer and winter. The winter here is unlike a European winter and you would not need heavy winter coats or jackets, although there are strong chilly winds. Annual average rainfall for Melbourne is around 650mm.

CHILDREN
Education
When it comes to education, Melbourne offers a host of choices. The city was given a perfect score for education from the Economist Intelligence Unit's Global Liveability Survey 2017. From childcare, kindergartens, primary and secondary education, you can decide on the type of environment suitable for your child and the costs involved.

Playgroup Victoria (www.playgroup.org.au) will provide you with a list of playgroups to choose from and the costs. You can obtain a list of kindergartens in your suburb from the local council. It is best to register early to secure a place in a popular one. I had to get my sister-in-law's help to register my child at kindergarten before we arrived so that my child could

get admission. The eastern suburbs is popular with many migrants and competition for admission to state schools is keen.

The education system in Australia consists of three stages: preschool, primary and high school, and tertiary. It is not compulsory to send your child to kindergarten or preschool. However both public and private schools offer a preparatory grade to prepare your children for school.

Primary school education is compulsory for children between the ages of 6 and 15. The final years, Year 11 and 12 are for the preparation of the Victorian Certificate of Education (VCE) which enables entry to university. Alternative assessment programmes such as the International Baccalaureate are also available at some schools.

There is a choice of private and public schools. It is similar to the British system of education but not as elitist. Public schools are state run and affordable to all. They are coeducational schools while private schools are privately run and may be single-gender or have religious affiliations. The choices are plentiful as there are more than 500 private schools and more than 16,500 government schools. You can even choose to homeschool your child but you must register with the Victorian Registrations and Qualifications Authority.

English is the medium of instruction in Australia and even non-English speaking migrants will find that their children will soon learn English. There are many schools and private organisations which run intensive English language training programmes. Some of them are not for profit and migrants can avail themselves of these services. There are a range of support services to help students settle into school: buddy systems, counselling and support for students with learning difficulties. For more information, visit the Department of Education and Training website at www.education.vic.gov.au.

Entertainment

Entertainment for children is varied. Other than movies at the cinema, there are exciting activities for the young such as free entry to the zoo on weekends, exhibitions, family friendly festivals such as Moomba, interactive exhibitions like Artvo and Art Play, and adventure rooms like Escape Room and Escape Hunt. There is a Comedy Club for kids every Easter. Find out more at whatson.melbourne.vic.gov.au.

BANKING AND TAXES
Banking

There is a myriad of banks to choose from if you wish to open an account. The big four banks are ANZ, Commonwealth Bank of Australia, National Australian Bank (NAB) and Westpac. These banks have a migrant service with dedicated multilingual staff to help you.

Whether you are a student, working in Melbourne or a migrant, the procedure to open an account is straightforward. Even before you arrive in Melbourne, you can open an account online or through a phone call, arrange with your local bank which has ties with a Melbourne bank to help you open an account.

Once you are in Melbourne, all you need to do is to visit a local branch with your passport. You may also need your plane ticket or copy of the bank's account-opening letter. Once your account is opened, you will receive a debit card and a PIN.

If you are opening an account six weeks after you first arrive, you would need to provide more forms of identification such as an overseas credit card, student identification if relevant and a letter proving your residence in Melbourne. This may include your birth certificate, marriage certificate, driver's licence, or perhaps a credit card from your country of origin. These documents are used to meet the 100 points check, a personal identification test adopted by the

Australian Government to combat financial transaction fraud.

There are many types of accounts to choose from depending on purpose. Students who only require a basic account to pay their expenses from may choose a transaction account with low management fees. This account allows you to withdraw money for your daily expenses. A working professional might desire a more elaborate account, though there's a higher management fee. Drawing from your account is easy as the city offers more than 100 Automated Teller Machines (ATM) to make deposits and withdrawals. There may be charges if you use another bank's ATM.

In terms of managing your account, there are several options. Internet banking is now popular as it allows you to view your statement, transfer money and pay bills in the privacy of your home. For those who prefer face-to-face contact, you can visit the bank for these transactions although some banks do charge for such services. For more detailed banking information, visit the respective banks' websites.

Business Banking

If you need to open a business banking account, apart from personal identification, you may need to offer details of your business structure, Australian Business Number (ABN) or Australian Company Number (CAN), business or company address and details such as shareholders and directors of the company. Different banks offer different products, interest rates, fees and charges. For more details, see www.business. vic.gov.au.

Taxes

The tax system in Australia is complex and this will apply to Melbourne. The tax year runs from 1 July to 30 June. For the best advice, it is recommended that you engage a tax advisor or accountant, after having read through the information found in the Australian Taxation Office and Australian Government Office websites.

The individual tax rate is progressive:

Taxable income	Tax on this income
$0 – A$18,200	Nil
A$18,201 – A$37,000	19c for each A$1 over A$18,200
A$37,001 – A$87,000	A$3,572 plus 32.5c for each A$1 over A$37,000
A$87,001 – A$180,000	A$19,822 plus 37c for each A$1 over A$87,000
A$180,001 and over	A$54,232 plus 45c for each A$1 over A$180,000

The corporate tax rate for base rate entities (defined as a company which has an aggregated turnover of less than A$25 million for the income year, and is carrying on a business) is 27.5 per cent and for companies other than that is 30 per cent. If you run your own business and employ staff, there are requirements which must be met such as minimum pay, withholding PAYG tax, superannuation and environmental safety requirements.

All employers must provide superannuation which are retirement savings for their employees. It is an additional 9.5 per cent of their wages which must be deposited into an approved superannuation fund. The ASIC website provides useful information on superannuation. More detailed information can be found at www.liveinmelbourne.vic.gov.au.

SHOPPING
Fashion
You cannot live in Melbourne and not visit what is affectionately known as "Chaddy". Chadstone Shopping

Centre is a shopping centre located in the south-eastern suburb of Malvern East. It is huge! I cannot think of any shopaholic who would not want to spend a few hours here. It offers more than 530 stores with free parking. Be warned, it gets awfully busy and more than 60,000 visitors have graced its halls in a single day. Major Australian retailers like Myer and David Jones, supermarkets such as Coles, Woolworths and Aldi, discount stores such as Kmart and Target all sit together under its roof.

High end fashion stores are found at Collins Street and Chapel Street at South Yarra; Australian fashion at Gertrude Street Fitzroy; and bridal wear in High Street Armadale.

For a feel of old Melbourne, you must visit the Block Arcade, a heritage shopping arcade in the central business district of Melbourne. The newcomer, Emporium Melbourne, opened in 2014, is a luxury shopping centre on the corner of Lonsdale and Swanston streets. Take a walk down Collins Street and you will find Bourke Street Mall where you can spend a few hours shopping. Budget fashion is found at Bridge Road and Direct Factory Outlets at South Wharf and Moorabin. Vintage fashion is located on Sydney Road in Brunswick.

Supermarkets Coles and Woolworths, Aldi, a German budget supermarket and Independent Grocers Australia (IGA) can be found in major suburbs. Dan Murphy's, Liquorland (run by Coles) and BWS (run by Woolworths) sell alcohol.

Fresh Produce Markets

Dandenong market offers spices and all things nice from Afghanistan, India and Ethiopia at cheap prices. Springvale and Little Saigon Market located at Footscray sells seafood, meats, Asian vegetables such as bean sprouts and dragon fruit and Vietnamese food like *pho* and *banh mi pate*.

Prahran Market at South Yarra is where trendy foodies go looking for goose, exotic nuts, and mushrooms. Preston

Market is where you find reasonably priced Mediterranean, Middle-eastern and Asian food. Queen Victoria Market is still a favourite of city dwellers—you can still find deli goods, fresh meat and seafood, vegetables and fruits. Farmer's markets or flea markets are usually organised by local councils over the weekend. You can find a farmer's market near you where you can enjoy fresh produce, home cooked pies, chutneys and relish.

Online Shopping
Go to www.finder.com.au for a guide on online shopping for fashion, health and beauty, home and garden, food and drink, electronics, books and gifts.

Budget Shops
Daiso, located at the Emporium, is a discount variety chain that offers cheap but pretty designs for homeware, crockery, tableware, and stationery. Made in Japan, located in South Melbourne, sells imported quality tableware and homeware from Japan.

Terra Madre, located in Northcote, sells bulk food at reasonable prices: they offer fresh fruit and vegetables, dairy, meat and bread to grocery items like cereals, grains, sauces, oils, flour, nuts, seeds, as well as gluten-free, dairy-free, organic treats.

HEALTH INSURANCE
Public Health Cover
Australia has two national programmes to reduce medical costs: Medicare and the Pharmaceutical Benefits Scheme. Medicare is Australia's public healthcare system. Only eligible Australian residents (either Australia and NZ citizens or permanent residents) receive free treatment in a public hospital as well as reduced costs for out-of-hospital care.

Those who hold temporary visas are ineligible for Medicare unless you are from countries like UK, Finland, Ireland Belgium, which have a Reciprocal Health Care Agreement with Australia.

The Pharmaceutical Benefits Scheme provides for more affordable prescription medicine. Eligible Medicare residents qualify for these benefits.

Private Health Insurance

You can get private health insurance in Australia for hospital cover, treatment cover (also known as extras cover) and ambulance cover, either as single policies or combined policies. For wider coverage and benefits, many opt for private health insurance if they can afford it. The popular insurance companies are BUPA, Medibank and HCF. Check out the Australian Medical Association and Private Health Insurance websites for more details.

Private Hospital Cover

This allows you to choose your doctor, surgeon and hospital, with access to private hospitals and reduced waiting times for elective surgery. Extras in private health insurance include services such as dental, chiropractic, home nursing, podiatry, physiotherapy, occupational therapy, speech and eye therapy, glasses and contact lenses, and prostheses.

Temporary residents and migrants must have health insurance for the duration of their stay in Australia. If your current health fund is a member of the International Federation of Health Plans (IFHP), you may be able to transfer to an Australian fund, without penalty, and with a similar level of cover.

Lifetime Health Cover
The Commonwealth government has introduced a Lifetime Health Cover which increases the private health insurance premium by 2 per cent for every year you remain uninsured after 30 years.

Ambulance Cover
Ambulance costs are expensive. A single trip can cost between A$900 to more than A$5,500 if an air ambulance is necessary. By becoming a member of Ambulance Victoria, the cost is A$43.80 for single cover and A$87.60 for family cover for one year. Private health insurance too may cover part or all of your ambulance costs, depending on the policy.

TRANSPORT
Melbourne has a reasonably reliable public transport system, with trains, trams and buses. The metropolitan train network is operated by Metro while V/Line operates Victoria's regional public transport.

Melbourne is spread out and it is best to drive if you need to travel long distances for work or school. While you can depend on public transportation such as trains, buses or trams, you may find that these do not always run to schedule in the weekends or off-peak hours.

The good news is that you only need to purchase one card, a myki card, regardless of whether you wish to travel on a tram or bus. This plastic card uses a touch on/touch off process similar to other public transport ticketing systems around the world. The full fare is A$6 for those aged 19 years and above while concession holders pay half price. For details visit www.myki.com.au.

For tourists, the myki Explorer is a ready-to-use card for one day's unlimited travel on public transport in Melbourne. The pack includes a ready-to-use myki card with one day's unlimited travel in metropolitan Melbourne, handy maps (train, tram, city centre), special offers from 16 popular Melbourne and regional attractions with information on how to get there by public transport, and a souvenir wallet.

Taxis and Ubers

You can hire a taxi whether in the city or outside by phone, online, app or on the road. The taxis provide a metered service which is usually more expensive compared to Ubers.

Buying a Car

Buying a car in Melbourne is affordable, especially secondhand, and you have a range of choices.

There are many car dealers selling new and used cars so make sure you are dealing with a licensed dealer. If you decide to buy a car by private sale or auction, be aware that

the car must have a Certificate of Roadworthiness and that ownership must be transferred within two weeks of purchase with VicRoads. The Royal Automobile Club of Victoria website (www.racv.com.au) provides useful information on car prices and the costs of maintaining a car.

Some car sale websites to visit are drive.com.au and carsales.com.au.

Car Hire

When you arrive at the airport, you can arrange to hire a car from a car rental agency. There are many models to choose from ranging from four-wheel drives and sedans to motorhomes or UTEs. Depending on the type of car and days of hire, the cost will differ. Younger drivers have to pay a higher price. If you drop the car off at a different location too, you may have to pay extra. It is necessary to obtain insurance for the driver which is included in the rental costs. All drivers must have a driving licence and comply with the agency's terms and conditions of hire.

Driving in Melbourne

If you wish to drive in Melbourne, you need to have a valid driving licence. If your overseas driver's licence is from a recognised country or a country where driving experience is recognised, you may not need to take a test. There is a list of 27 countries that includes Singapore, the UK and the US, where driving licences are recognised and a list of 16 countries where driver experience is recognised. If your license is from a country other than these two categories, you would need to arrange to convert your licence by first sitting for a Road Law Knowledge test and Hazard Perception test before the drive test. If you need an interpreter for a test, you'll need to book your test at the VicRoads Customer Service Centre where you are taking the test.

Melbourne has catered to its multi-ethnic population by providing videos, handbooks and fact sheets in a variety of languages on how to get a driving licence, buy and register a car and ensure road safety. Visit www.vicroads.gov.au.

Dealing with Accidents

In the unfortunate event that you are involved in an accident you must stop your vehicle. This requirement applies even if no one is hurt. You should exchange details with the other driver or the owner of any property that is damaged. Do note that it is an offence to leave the scene of a vehicle accident without doing this.

If the police are called and attend the accident scene, they will interview the people involved and any other witnesses, and may even charge the driver(s). If the police wish to test you as a driver for alcohol or other drugs, you are required to comply as it is an offence to refuse the test.

Generally the person who causes a crash is responsible for the damage caused. You can claim for the cost of repairs to a damaged car through your insurance company or through the courts, if necessary.

In the event that another person's property is damaged or the other party failed to stop or give their details, the accident may be reported to the police. Accidents which do not involve injury to a person are usually not reported to the police.

Keeping a record of the details of the accident such as the time date and location, speed, weather, and witness details are important. It will help you write your statement. You should report the accident to your insurance company for their record whether or not you wish to make an insurance claim.

In the event that a person is injured, the Transport Accident Commission (TAC) will be involved as insurance for personal injury is included in the cost of vehicle registration. The TAC will pay the medical costs of the injured person(s).

TELECOMMUNICATIONS

There are 4 major mobile phone providers in Melbourne: Telstra, Optus, Vodafone and Virgin Mobile. You can purchase a package deal which includes data, handset and pre-agreed monthly usage, a contract for a fixed period of time (18 or 24 months) a prepaid plan which limits you to a credit limit with capped inclusions (where you receive a text message when you are reaching your usage limit) and data packages for frequent internet use. Landlines are hardly used except by older people and this is usually packaged within a Data Internet plan.

Mobile Phone Etiquette

Mobile phone etiquette in Australia differs from Asia where you can see people texting or taking calls even when they are face to face with another person. In Melbourne, it is considered rude and you should give your full attention when you are face-to-face with others.

Avoid talking at the top of your voice or yelling when you

take a call, especially on public transport. Aussies are polite but they would be uncomfortable with loud mobile phone conversations on the train.

Always ask to be excused from a meeting or a conversation if you need to text or take a call. If a call is important, apologise and ask permission before accepting it.

Make sure your mobile phone is on silent when you are attending an event in a public place, at a movie or concert, as a sign of respect for others.

GENERAL SAFETY

In 2017, The Economist Intelligence Unit ranked Melbourne among the top ten safest cities in the world in their Safe Cities Index. However during busy festive periods such as Christmas or Grand Final Day, there is a danger of pickpockets around Flinders Street—the station as well as in the Docklands area. While the main shopping area within the city, that is, Swanston Street, is full of pedestrians and trams during the day, it does get quiet in the night. The red light district near King's Street is an area which should be avoided at night.

Women's Safety

Like any other city in the world, women are advised to stay vigilant and cautious when travelling in the night in Melbourne. The rape and murder of a 22-year-old female comedian in a Melbourne park in mid-June 2018 has raised public debate on how safe Melbourne is for women at night.

Plan International Australia, an independent development and humanitarian organisation focusing on children's rights and gender issues, created a digital mapping tool in 2017 identifying safe and unsafe places for women commuters when using the public transport system at night. They identified safe places which are well lit and where female commuters had positive experiences, and unsafe places where women have experienced fearful situations.

Monash University analysed the data in 2018 and found that 14 per cent of respondents expressed concerns and fears about safety while using trains and trams offered by the city's public transport system. There were fears of being sexually harassed or assaulted while using public transport, especially for women under the age of 30. For those who drive or take a taxi or Uber, there has been less negative publicity regarding women's safety.

CHAPTER 6

FOOD AND
ENTERTAINING

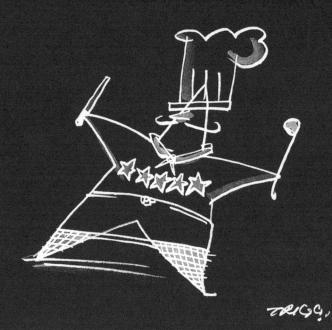

> *With TV cooking shows and celebrity chefs as popular as ever, it's almost a matter of pride for many people to visit the latest restaurant or café before their friends: home-delivered pizza just won't cut it anymore!*

— Norman Morris, Roy Morgan Research

Cosmopolitan Melbourne boasts an incredible array of international cuisines, so any visitor is spoilt for choice. The Australian obsession with food is evident in the reality television shows such as *My Kitchen Rules* and *MasterChef Australia*. *MasterChef Australia*, based on the UK *Masterchef*, is the most watched competitive cooking television series in Australia. *MasterChef Australia*'s 2018 winner is Singapore-born Sashi Cheliah who impressed the judges with his cooking skills and a Singaporean-influenced menu.

My Kitchen Rules produced by Seven Studios is a cooking competition where teams of everyday Australians cook a three course menu designed to impress the judges and their fellow teams. The series has been sold across more than 160 countries worldwide. The final competition between two finalist teams is telecast to as many as 1.9 million viewers and the winners get A$250,000.

Stephanie Alexander is a Melbourne-based cook, restauranteur and author. In 2014, she was appointed an Officer of the Order of Australia for distinguished service to education through the design and establishment of schools-based learning programmes promoting improved food habits and eating choices for children. She established the Stephanie Alexander Kitchen Garden Foundation in 2004, a not-for-profit organisation dedicated to supporting schools introducing kitchen gardens into primary schools.

COFFEE CULTURE

Melbourne is famous for its coffee culture brought by the Italians in the early 1930s. Classics include lattes, cappuccinos, ristrettos and espressos with dairy or non-dairy substitutes like soy or almond milk. Cold press or cold brews are also popular. Teas too are not limited to black teas or herbal teas, and chai lattes and turmeric lattes are new staples.

The coffee culture is so prevalent that you will find Melburnians having a coffee any time of the day: after shopping, in the afternoon or at dinner. The average office worker has one to two coffees a day and office meetings usually serve coffee. Everyone has their own favourite coffee haunt. Popular ones in the city are Brother Baba Budan, Patricia Coffee Brewers and Industry Beans.

The espresso was invented in 1901 by Luigi Bezzera in Milan. In the 1930s, the first espresso machine made its way to Melbourne at Cafe Florentino (now a restaurant called Grossi Florentino) on Bourke Street. Grinder's Coffee on Lygon Street is also a Melburnian icon as the café is recognised for introducing good Italian coffee to the city. It was and still is a place when Melburnians could enjoy a good cup of Italian coffee.

Starbucks attempted to break into the coffee market in Melbourne, but by 2008, was forced to close 70 per cent of its cafés. Melburnians know their coffee well and only the best Italian espresso will do!

Grinders Coffee

Giancarlo Giusti and Rino Benassi, the founders of Grinders, wanted to bring European coffee to Melbourne. Giancarlo had purchased a large red grinder for just £1. Operating from the store, he roasted and ground coffee beans, and began selling coffee in 1962. It became a hit with Melburnians, in particular the university students who were studying in the vicinity. Today, the shop still has a coffee roasting facility at the back and the aroma of the freshly ground beans still draws visitors who walk along Lygon Street.

EVERYDAY FARE

Walking through a supermarket aisle, you can see the influence of multiculturalism with rotis from Malaysia, frozen steamed buns from China, an assortment of breads and cereals, Italian fresh and dried pastas, Greek yoghurts, ice creams, desserts, meats and seafood. The chilled section has deli foods with assortments of cheeses, hams and salami. For the health conscious, you can find organic eggs, meats and fresh produce.

A popular, trendy Melburnian breakfast is smashed avo' (avocado—Aussies love to abbreviate everything). Melbourne has moved past traditional bacon and eggs to fusion foods: fried egg on crispy Korean rice cakes, chilli scrambled eggs, polenta porridge, cuttlefish kimchi. Brunch too goes fusion: poached eggs and dukkha spices, ferrero rocher pancakes, pork belly and duck. You might even find some fusion cafés serving Asian rotis or congee.

If you are eating at home, a popular accompaniment with your toast is Vegemite. A true Aussie won't leave home without it. Many Melburnians are health conscious and you find that Weetbix is a popular breakfast option for many children as well as adults. A popular commercial ditty on television goes: "Aussie kids are Weetbix kids".

Vegemite on toast

Lunch is usually a quick meal for many. For the health conscious, it could be a variety of salads, quinoa or rice bowls or sandwiches. Vietnamese *pho* and rice rolls have become a staple for many Melburnians and for those who like spice, Malaysian *laksa* is also popular. Sushi, too, is popular and available in most shopping malls or at the supermarket. *Yum cha* or *dim sum* is popular too but the quality and selection does not compare with those found in Asia.

FOOD FESTIVALS

A good showcase of Melburnians' love for food is at one of the several food festivals the city hosts. The Melbourne Food and Wine Festival is an annual event that has been celebrated since 1993. It is a feast for gourmet lovers and extends over a week in locations from restaurants and laneways to rooftops and hills. A gastronomic delight to locals and tourists, the event has seen world-class chefs such as Heston Blumenthal, Nigella Lawson and Jamie Oliver gracing the occasion.

The World's Longest Lunch features an elaborate spread of food along a 500 m-long table set for 1,700 diners along the banks of the Maribyrnong River. The three-course menu has chefs from all over the world, bringing exotic flavours into a modern-Australian feast.

There are also regional celebrations in areas like Daylesford and Port Fairy.

COSMOPOLITAN OFFERINGS

Due to the diverse society in Melbourne, there are different suburbs that specialise in different ethnic food. Greek restaurants, cafés and bakeries can be found in Oakleigh, Italian fare on Lygon Street, Vietnamese food in Springvale, Chinese food in Box Hill and Glen Waverley, and Sri Lankan and Indian food in Glen Waverley and Dandenong. In Melbourne today, you would find a variety of foods in the food court of a shopping mall, from burgers and sandwiches to Asian and European fare.

INDIGENOUS FOOD

Many restaurants in Melbourne offer native Australian food either in their menu or use such native ingredients in the preparation of the meals. The use of native ingredients such as King George Whiting, mud crabs, spanner crabs and macadamias, gives the food a distinctive Australian flavour. Charcoal Lane is a popular restaurant cum social enterprise set up by Mission Australia which has a menu of indigenous foods cooked by budding indigenous chefs. The restaurant provides traineeships for young and aspiring Aboriginal and Torres Strait Islander chefs.

Altair Restaurant in Warrandyte uses indigenous ingredients such as berries, stinging nettle and bush tomatoes in their fish and meat dishes.

FAST FOOD DELIVERY

In addition to the usual fast food delivery from KFC, McDonalds and Crust, Melbourne offers food delivery from fine dining restaurants such as the Press Club, Hellenic Republic and Gazi through Uber Eats, Deliveroo, and Foodora.

BREAD

Melbourne is home to a variety of breads from supermarket brands to artisanal breads to traditional Greek, Lebanese and Turkish bread like *pita* and *pide*.

The Lune Croissanterie, located in Fitzroy, specialises in traditional and more modern croissants like cruffins (an original cross between a croissant and muffin) and twice-baked croissants. I visited the bakery to find streams of tourists from China and Indonesia sampling the croissants. While the croissants were tasty, paying A$9 for a ham and cheese croissant was expensive!

Baker D. Chirico is known for whole wheat bread which is not only tasty but nutritious. Their hot cross buns are an Easter favourite. Wild Life Bakery is home to vegetarian delights like toasties and breads with caramelised onion, house-made kimchi, comté and cheddar.

Supermarkets offer breads from a wide range of different commercial bakers: wholemeal bread, whole wheat bread, high-fibre, low glycaemic index, prebiotic bread, cholesterol-reducing bread, rye sourdough and gluten free breads.

Franchises such as Baker's Delight also offer breads to indulge your sweet tooth, savoury breads and healthy breads like high-fibre and low-glycaemic index (GI).

For more traditional breads, you can visit bakeries like Babka, an Eastern European bakery known for its vegetable loaf, Glicks', a Jewish bakery which serves challah bread (a traditional kosher braided egg loaf) and Woodfrog Bakery for its *soir* (a blend of organic sourdough, wholemeal wheat, rye and malted barley).

CHEESE

Cheese is popular with Melburnians and there are home grown varieties and imported cheeses to choose from. In Victoria, Yarra Valley cheeses, Main Ridge at Mornington and Cloud 9 in Daylesford are some of the local cheeses. You can savour your cheeses at boutique cheese stores, cellar doors, bars and restaurants.

Cheese Shops

Miss Gourmet & Co in Hawthorn originated from Western Australia back in the 1960s and offers a goat cheese, Le Delice De Bourgogne, made of triple cream and cow's milk with butterfat. The Holy Goat La Lune, a goat cheese, is made on the Sutton Grange Organic Farm in Victoria, in a traditional French soft curd style.

DOC Delicatessen at Carlton brings in Italian cheeses and their Black Truffled Pecorino, a sheep milk cheese from Tuscany, is combined with black truffle shavings. DOC Pizza & Mozzarella offers a wide selection of post-meal cheeses, buffalo mozzarella, burrata and gorgonzola.

Milk the Cow Licensed Fromagerie is a late night cheese bar located in St Kilda and Carlton. They offer over 180 different cheeses from all around the world in a 6 m-long cheese cabinet which are matched to wines, cocktails, beer,

whisky, sake and more. They run classes and offer tasting plates. There is a huge variety including Melbourne creations like the Bella Vitano Espresso, a cheese coated in ground coffee beans and Langres, a washed-rind cow's milk cheese with a soft, creamy centre.

Harper & Blohm Cheese Shop is a popular cheese shop since 2014 located in Essendon offering farmhouse and artisan cheeses from Australia, the UK, Europe and the US. The cheeses are selected from Neal's Yard Dairy of London. It also offers a local range of charcuterie, biscuits and accompaniments. An online shop has been open since 2017. Prom Country Venus Blue is a blue cheese made from ewes milk from Gippsland as well as a Yarra Valley Dairy creation known as the Stone & Crow Night Walker, a full-bodied handmade washed rind cheese.

The Cheese Cellar in Spring Street Grocer is Australia's first underground cheese maturation cellar offering farmhouse and artisan cheeses sourced locally and overseas. The basement space can be booked for cheese-themed cocktail and dinner parties. The selection of cheeses are presented in a temperature-controlled room behind glass.

The Cheese Room at Richmond Hill Cafe and Larder which was originally started by Stephanie Alexander is a Melbourne institution. It offers temperature-controlled cheeses with wine.

Gazi was lauded by chef Nigella Lawson for their feta chips, (chips tossed through garlic oil and topped with feta). "These chips were absolutely worth flying the 10,496.05 miles for," she wrote in *The Guardian* in 2017.

The French Shop which is located in Queen Victoria Market's Deli Hall has imported and local cheese while the Cheese Shop Deli in Prahran specialises in a wide range of Australian and French cheeses. Cornelius Cheesemongers is an online cheese experience opened in 2010 which sells farmhouse and artisan cheeses from Australia, the UK, Europe & the USA. You can learn how to make your own cheese at Henry and the Fox's cheese-making masterclass.

To top it all, a high tea known as High Cheese is offered at the Westin Melbourne for cheese lovers where both sweet and savoury cheese dishes are offered.

WINE

Melbourne is located in the state of Victoria and the Yarra Valley is known as a wine region where a variety of wines are made. Most Melburnians enjoy their wine and would have made at least one visit to the Yarra Valley in their lifetime. The Yara Valley climate and soil produces world-class Chardonnay and Pinot Noir as well as Cabernet Sauvignon and Shiraz.

If you are new to Melbourne and not accustomed to drinking wines or knowing your wines, what follows is a brief introduction to some common wines.

White

Chardonnay

The grape variety grown in the cooler climates such as the Mornington Peninsula are lighter and more acidic compared to those grown in warmer climate which has a richer flavour. The wine has a citrus and fruity flavour. The wine may be paired with chicken, pork and seafood.

Sauvignon Blanc

Sauvignon Blanc can range in flavour from citrus to tropical fruit. Wineries in Gembrook Hill and Coldstream Hill in the Yarra Valley produce this wine. Aged Sauvignon Blanc has a creamy flavour may be paired with lemon curd, cocktail and party foods.

Pinot Gris/Pinot Grigio

The Pinot Grigio is a light dry wine while the Pinot Gris has a richer, fruity flavour. Both wines are grown from the same grape variety and grown in the Mornington Peninsula. The wine may be paired with Italian food.

Sparkling Wine

Premium styles of sparkling wine like Sparkling Chardonnay and Pinot Noir are found in the Yarra Valley. Sparkling Chardonnay are wines with a higher proportion of Chardonnay and a relatively shorter aging process and are light and crisp, while the Sparkling Pinor Noirs are richer and full bodied.

Rosé

Produced in the Yarra Valley tends to be salmon to pink in colour and is fruity.

Red
Pinot Noir

Pinot Noir means black pine'. Although the grape variety originated in Burgundy, it is grown in the Mornington Peninsula as well as the Yarra Valley. The notes range from violet to berries. The wine may be paired with cheeses, game, Italian risotto and pizza.

Cabernet Sauvignon

Cabernet Sauvignon is produced in the warmer areas of the Yarra Valley. The wine itends to be full bodied and richly perfumed with eucalyptus and fruity tones. The wine may be paired with red meat.

Shiraz/Syrah

The Yarra "Syrah" is more lighter and has savoury characteristics of olive or fermented meat flavours while the more full-bodied Shiraz has a more elegant taste. The variety is grown in Heathcote, Victoria.

Other Varieties

Lighter bodies reds such as Grenache and medium bodied reds such as Merlot and Sangiovese are also produced.

Domaine Valley, Oakridge, Yering Station, Coombe Valley, De Bortoli and Rochford wines are some of the regional wines available in Melbourne.

DINING AND ENTERTAINING ETIQUETTE
Wine and BYO

Ten years ago, it was customary to bring your own bottle to a restaurant without any corkage charge. Today, with more gourmet cafés and restaurants, prices have increased

View from Paringa Estate Winery

and only some allow you to BYO—Bring Your Own. You are advised to check with the restaurant before you bring a bottle. When serving alcohol, it is a legal requirement that a standard pour of 150 ml is served, with no generous overpouring of drinks. The drink driving laws are strict so if you drink, don't drive, as there will be booze buses and police stops along your journey back.

Sharing dishes is a new norm in Melbourne. Whether Asian, Italian, Greek, Middle Eastern or Latin American, most restaurants now allow sharing or offer sharing platters.

Attire
Unless the website indicates formal wear, most Australian restaurants are happy with smart casual. Although Aussies may seem laid back, you should not be sloppily dressed. Check with the restaurant for its dress code.

Seating
If there is a "Wait to be seated" sign, you should observe it. If you are expecting a group of friends, it is polite to wait for them before being seated, and for everyone to be served before eating.

Use of Mobile Phones

In the digital age, many diners bring their mobile phones to restaurants. However it would be rude to put them on the table and start texting when dining with others. If you need to take an urgent call, excuse yourself before you do so.

Bills

You have to request for the bill to be brought to the table as this is not automatic. The normal custom is a tip of 10 per cent. If you use a credit or debit card, you can add the tip on your payment.

If you are with a group and choose to split a bill, it is best to have decided beforehand to either split the bill equally or in specific amounts. Some restaurants have apps which allow you to do so.

Reservations

The popular time for dinner reservations is 6:30pm. So if you are trying to make a reservation at a popular restaurant, book a later sitting.

Table Manners

Follow the Australian style of placing your napkin on your lap when you sit down and resting your cutlery at the 4:20 position when you're finished.

If you are celebrating a special occasion such as a birthday or anniversary, you can bring a gift whether the celebration is at a restaurant or in a home. Common gifts for the host of a dinner party are flowers, chocolates, potted plants, bottles of wine, decorative candles and soaps.

TYPICAL MELBURNIAN FOOD

Gelato, or Italian ice-cream without the calories, is available at most shopping centres and beach shops. A favourite brand is Gelato Messina which offers 40 traditional and modern flavours such as watermelon and lime granite. Vegan and gluten-free options are easily available.

There is no end to **coffee** shops and cafés. Popular favourites include Market Lane Coffee which can be found in Queen Vic market and South Yarra, Seven Seeds in Carlton and Industry Beans in Fitzroy.

Pavlova, a meringue-based dessert named after the Russian ballerina Anna Pavlova, is popular at Christmas and served with fruit and whipped cream. It has a crisp crust but is soft and light inside.

Vegemite, the thick, black food spread made from leftover brewer's yeast extract with various vegetable and spice additives, was developed by Cyril Percy Callister in Melbourne in 1922.

Tim Tam, Australia's famous chocolate biscuit made by Arnott's, an Australian company, is traditionally made of two malted biscuits separated by a light chocolate cream filling and coated in a thin layer of textured chocolate. New flavours

Vegemite ice cream

such as dark chocolate, chocolate mint, salted caramel and vanilla, coconut and lychee, and black forest have emerged.

Fish and chips, a favourite with Melburnians as a takeaway, for weekends or at the beach. There is even an award for Victoria's Best Fish and Chips annually.

Vanilla slice, also known as the mille-feuille, custard slice, or the Napoleon, is French in origin. The Great Australian Vanilla Slice Triumph has been hotly contested since 1998. There have been creative variations such as pina colada and cherry.

Souvlaki, a Greek pita sandwich filled with roasted meat (either lamb or chicken from the spit), lettuce and tomato, topped with *tzatziki,* parsley, onion, mustard or mayonnaise, is a popular favourite for a quick lunch, at sporting events or after-drinks supper.

Pho, a Vietnamese rice noodle soup with herbs served with beef or chicken.

Food trucks, the hugely popular American food trend, has landed in Melbourne. The choices are plenty: White Guy Cooks Thai for Asian food, Dos Diablos for Mexican, Gumbo Kitchen for New Orleans food, Little Mushroom Company for vegetarians and the Brulee Cart for desserts.

Meat pies are an old-fashioned Australian favourite especially with older Australians who ate them as children at meals, at a footy or cricket match, at children's parties and afternoon tea. The pies come in various sizes, from party pies to the regular size and with all kinds of savoury and gourmet fillings. Some of the choices are Angus beef and red wine, beef and Guinness, lamb curry, and kangaroo. Four'N Twenty is Australia's most famous pie maker and the frozen variety is available in supermarkets.

DRINKING

While lockout laws are in place in NSW and Queensland, Melbourne does not have them, after they were tried and rejected in Victoria. The Victorian Premier Daniel Andrews has stated that Melbourne's late night economy is worth hundreds of millions of dollars and provides employment to a few

A food truck offering Spanish tapas and churros

thousand. However, Peter Miller, a Deakin University professor and co-author of a study on drunkenness, has found that drunkenness in Australian pubs and clubs has increased as revellers partied into the early hours of the morning.

There are rules in place to keep the community safe and promote responsible drinking, especially late at night. The City of Melbourne's Activities Local Law 2009 bans the consumption of alcohol in public places in the Central Business District 24 hours a day, 365 days a year. This ban is also in force during New Year's Eve, the Melbourne Moomba Festival (Labour Day long weekend) and the Australian Grand Prix. Alcohol is also banned at major events in the streets and reserves of Carlton, in the area bounded by Victoria Parade and Swanston, Elgin and Nicholson streets. Only licensed outdoor dining is unaffected. However it is legal to drink in public parks either as an individual or in groups of 50 people or less.

UNIQUE BARS

Mention wine bars and most people will recognise the iconic Jimmy Watson's Wine Bar located in Lygon Street, Carlton in Melbourne. Jim Watson is credited as the Melburnian who promoted social drinking of wine by both sexes. The first bar was opened at JC Watson Wine Merchants in 1935. At that time, it was mostly Australian men who were seen in public drinking beer. Hardly any women were seen drinking in public. He introduced table wine to Melbournian couples at his bar. From 1940 he organised trips to vineyards in an effort to educate customers on wine. He selected a "hogshead" (a cask) of his favourite wine styles and bottled them for sale at his bar. This tradition was marked with a Lion roaring over a barrel, which is still seen on the labels of Jimmy Watson wines today. After his death in 1962, a Jimmy Watson Memorial Trophy for the best young red wine still in barrel at the Royal Melbourne Show was established. It is still awarded today.

George's Bar, based on the character George Costanza in Seinfeld is located in Fitzroy, is filled with memorabilia from the show such as a Frogger machine, a vending machine filled only with Twix bars, and more than a few photos of Costanza plastered all over the walls. The bar serves cocktails like the Summer of George and Marisa Tomei. Definitely a must for a Seinfeld fan!

IceBar Melbourne is located in Brunswick and serves cocktails in ice glasses, set among a collection of ice sculptures. To withstand the freezing temperatures, guests are provided with snow capes, gloves and Ugg boots.

TRAPT Bar and Escape Room is a bar with a twist as it allows guests to solve a puzzle and relax after that with drinks such as wine, whisky, beers and cocktails.

Bar Americano is modelled on Americans bars in the 1920s, 1930s and 1940s. There's standing room for only about ten people, and serves classic cocktails and coffee.

Eau De Vie is a high-end bar which serves whiskies, cocktails and tasting menus. It has a hidden lounge behind a bookcase and is one of the busiest cocktail bars in Melbourne.

The Rum Diary Bar has a maritime theme and serves more than 200 types of rum. There are rum-based cocktails, and guests get to experience drinking below the deck.

Arbory Bar and Eatery is an outdoor eatery and beer garden located behind Flinders Street Station. A favourite with families, the office crowd and young adults, it boasts a view of the Yarra River. The bar is 120 m long and has a wide selection of wines, beers and cocktails. Some popular serves are the Espresso Martinis and Aperol Spritz.

Neighbourhood Wine, which was once the site for an illicit gambling den, is now a friendly bar and restaurant that offers a 20-page wine list of local and international wines as well as French-style cuisine in a cosy setting.

Whisky & Alement provides tasting sessions on a monthly

basis for whisky lovers. They have a takeaway licence for the specific purpose of selling single malt whisky.

The Shady Lady is a fun dive bar featuring vintage wallpaper, wood panelled walls, and tasselled lampshades over a long bar lined with stools. It is vegan- and dog-friendly.

Gin Palace, a basement cocktail bar decked with velvet, dim lighting and plush seats, has been around for twenty years and serves gin in the Central Business District.

CHAPTER 7

ENJOYING THE CULTURE

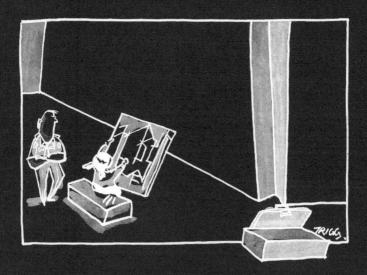

❛Melbourne is officially the sporting capital
of the world. ❜

— The Sydney Morning Herald, 21 April 2016

As Australia's cultural capital, UNESCO City of Literature and internationally recognised gathering place for street artists, musicians, entertainers and athletes, Melbourne plays host to many events throughout the year, from theatre, dance and musical to comedy and performance art at venues such as The Princess Theatre, Her Majesty's Theatre, Arts Centre and the Malthouse. In sports, it hosts the Australian Grand Prix, the Australian Open and the Melbourne Cup annually.

The Melbourne International Comedy Festival is held in April each year, bringing together world-class comedians from all over the world. What is attractive about the lineup is that there are comedians from different parts of the world which provide a rich variety to the audience, ensuring there is something for everyone.

ART GALLERIES AND EXHIBITIONS

In Melbourne there are more than a hundred galleries in total—private and public, big and small.

The National Gallery of Victoria is a world-class gallery which hosts Australian and international exhibitions. The NGV International is located on St Kilda Road while NGV Australia at Federation Square exhibits Australian Aboriginal art. Entrance to the galleries is free and you only need to pay for special exhibits. The Ian Potter Gallery at NGV Australia showcases Aboriginal art while ACMI (Australian Centre for the Moving Image) explores and promotes the moving image in all its forms—film, television and digital culture. Galleries at Flinders Lane also display indigenous art.

The National Gallery of Victoria

To experience art in the woods, you can visit the Heide Museum of Modern Art, the Linden Arts Centre or Herring Island for its sculptures and outdoor art. A visit to the Melbourne Museum provides an insight to the history of Melbourne, Aboriginal culture and science. Also on display is the stuffed skin of the famous racehorse Phar Lap, a New Zealand-born horse that won the Melbourne Cup in 1830. For younger children, seeing bugs and dinosaurs and watching a film on IMAX is a thrill. The Royal Exhibition Building, a World Heritage site, hosts trade fairs and exhibitions and is worth a visit for its Gothic and Rundbogenstil architectural styles.

I visited the NGV Triennial in January 2018 on St Kilda Road. It was an eclectic showcase of contemporary art and designs from over 100 artists and designers from 32 countries. Standouts included Yayoi Kusama's fun *Flower Obsession*, where visitors could stick a red flower sticker anywhere where they pleased; a Moroccan tea house; haute couture gowns by Chinese couturier Guo Pei; Ron Muick's thoughtful installation *Mass*, which consists of 100 larger-than-life skulls; a sleeping Buddha and Australian artist Ben Quilty's painting of a small orange lifejacket, representing the thousands of refugees who have died making the journey to Australia. It was a day well spent.

The Palais Theatre, a concert venue at St Kilda

BOOKS AND LITERATURE

Melbourne has been a UNESCO City of Literature since August 2008. It boasts bookstores, literary festivals, literary laneways and the iconic State Library of Victoria which sees a constant stream of students, writers, researchers and artists passing through its doors. Entry to the Library is free and it also houses a Centre for Youth Literature. Among the many writing festivals are Melbourne Writers' Festival, Overload Poetry Festival and the Emerging Writers' Festival.

The Wheeler Centre for Books, Writing and Ideas is a hub for writing and literature that houses the Victorian Writers' Centre and other key literary organisations. The writing cafés there play a part in creating a conducive environment for readers and writers. It is therefore not a surprise that many writers have resided in Melbourne, such as poet Dorothy Porter, feminist academic Germaine Greer and novelist Peter Carey. The latter was born outside Melbourne in Bacchus Marsh in Victoria and won the Man Booker prize in 2001 for his novel, *True History of the Kelly Gang*.

The seaside suburb of St Kilda is home to Phryne Fisher of the popular and internationally known television series, *Miss Fisher's Murder Mysteries*. Created by Melburnian author and

lawyer, Kerry Underwood, Miss Fisher's home is at 221B The Esplanade, St Kilda. Some murder scenes were set at a ghost train at Luna Park and the steps of St Kilda Town Hall.

In 2015, the Melbourne Walks Literary Tour was ranked ninth on Lonely Planet's list of the world's top ten literary tours. The tour explores literary highlights in the city centre such as the Nicholas Building with its "vertical laneway" of writers' studios, bookshops and publishers, and the Cole's Book Arcade, a Victorian-era bookshop which once spanned a city block.

Melbourne offers a range of bookshops from small, specialist, hole-in-the-wall laneway bookshops to larger chain ones which carry books on a plethora of issues. You will find a Readings bookshop in most inner city suburbs. Readings won the International Bookstore of the Year 2016. Avenue Bookstore, an award winning Australian bookseller for many years, also offers a wide selection of books together with events and readings.

CLASSICAL MUSIC

The world renowned Melbourne Symphony Orchestra (MSO) has concerts throughout the year and has a free performance at the Sidney Myer Music Bowl in summer. Established since 1906, it has its classical concerts at Hamer Hall at the Art Centre. It collaborates with the MSO Chorus and plays both classical and non-classical music.

The Melbourne Recital Centre is Melbourne's second largest auditorium for classical music and hosts hundreds of concerts. The repertoire is wide from baroque to popular music by both Australian and international artistes. It is home to Victorian and national chamber music ensembles, and is a venue for acclaimed companies such as the Australian Chamber Orchestra, Australian Brandenburg Orchestra, Australian National Academy of Music, Australian String

Quartet, Melbourne Chamber Orchestra, Melbourne Festival, Melbourne International Jazz Festival, Melbourne Symphony Orchestra, Musica Viva and Victorian Opera.

The architecture comprises two spaces: the Elisabeth Murdoch Hall and the Primrose Potter Salon. The former is a 1000-seat auditorium, lined with plywood panels of Australian Hoop pine timber and resembles the back of a beautiful instrument, while the latter is a 150-seat performance and event space where Melbourne composer Percy Grainger's 1937 graphic score, *Free Music No. 2,* is inscribed across the surface.

DANCE

The Melbourne Ballet Company and other contemporary dance companies such as Guerin Inc. and Chunky Move provide a lively dance scene. There are several dance competitions held in Melbourne through the year such as the Australian DanceSport Championships and Australian Tap Dance Competition.

The city is also home to the internationally renowned Australian Ballet, which partners with Orchestra Victoria to provide the music for all its Melbourne performances.

ABORIGINAL CULTURE

The Bunjilaka Melbourne Museum tells the story of Aboriginal Victoria from the time of Creation to modern times in the First Peoples exhibition. There is an etched zinc wall, *Wurreka* (which means "to speak" in Wemba Wemba, an extinct indigenous language), an artwork by Judy Watson, which has a total of 74 panels that reflect Aboriginal cultural heritage and landscapes of Victoria. Aboriginal Art usually takes the form of designs and symbols for waterholes, rainbows, fires or smoke, and illustrates the relationship between humans and the sacred earth. Such paintings which are referred to as

Theatre Etiquette

Whether you are attending a music performance, play, musical or ballet, there is social etiquette to be observed at these performances.

Buying Tickets

If you intend to buy tickets for a popular performance, it is advisable to make your booking early as there will be both local and foreign demand. Australians often travel interstate to watch performances and tourists are regular customers throughout the year.

Dress Codes

Most concert venues, theatres, arts centres or recital centres do not have a formal dress code and small casual attire would suffice. If it is the opening night, however, people do dress up and if you wish to enjoy the night, you should dress up too.

Punctuality

Arrive fifteen minutes earlier to start time at the latest. Most venues have a "lock out period", when doors lock at the start time. This information is usually printed on your ticket. You will be denied entry if you arrive late and the doors will only open at the next break.

Photo Taking and Video Recordings

Most venues do not allow the taking of photos, video and audio recordings as they are a direct violation of copyright laws. Set mobile phones on silent mode or switched off.

Cloaking

Most venues provide a free cloaking service for visitors attending concerts that is open before and after the performance ends. Do not bring any huge or odd sized bags or cases to the seats as there is limited space. These would need to be stored in the cloak room.

When to Applaud

While applause by the audience is appreciated, you need to know when to applaud depending on the type of performance. For example, in a classical music performance, there are conventions on when to do so. For example, you only applaud at the end of a symphony and not in between the movements. If you are unsure, follow the lead of the audience.

Attending with Children

Parents and guardians are responsible for their children's behaviour and should ensure that their children do not negatively impact the general enjoyment of the audience.

"The Dreaming" or "Dreamtime" are based on stories passed from the older generation. A visit to this museum is a good way to learn more about Aboriginal culture.

You can explore more Aboriginal culture at Gippsland's Bataluk Cultural Trail, Brambuk by Grampians National Park & Cultural Centre, or Baluk Arts on the Mornington Peninsula.

LIVEABLE MELBOURNE

Apart from a period of economic recession in 1991, Melbourne's economy has been stable and continues to grow. The city continues its urban renewal with new buildings, New York-style apartments and the upgrading of roads and transport. It is Australia's centre for world-class sports and cultural events in Australia, hosting the Australian Open, the Formula One Grand Prix, world-class musicals and pop concerts. Melbourne has also been described as "Australia's most stylish city after sunset". It is no wonder that *The Economist* has named Melbourne the world's most liveable city seven years in a row since 2011. Melbourne has its challenges with rising house prices and traffic congestion

as its population soars but this city still offers something for everyone. Since 2006, there has been an influx of migrants from China and India overtaking the Vietnamese and Sri Lankans and other ethnicities who came in the 1970s.

MELBOURNE'S LANEWAYS

Melbourne is famous for its lanes and alleys. There is much to discover while walking in the city and appreciating the street art that is creatively expressed on the walls of the laneways. Some notable laneways are the AC/DC Lane (named after Australía's favourite rock band), Cocker Alley and Hosier Lane.

AC/DC Lane is a narrow laneway that runs between Exhibition Street and Russell Street. Previously named Corporation Lane, it has been given new life with a grand opening by Melbourne's Lord Mayor in 2004.

Cocker Alley is a laneway south of Flinders Lane. At first sight it looks dingy but a Banksy painting known as *The Little Diver* was discovered there, only to later be defaced by vandals. It has since been recreated by a Melbourne artist and is now referred to as *The Little Diver Resurfaced*. There is also a 10-m decorated wall which depicts pairs of Australian fauna called *Neon Natives* by artist Reko Rennie.

Hosier Lane is Melbourne's most celebrated laneway for street art. Its cobbled streets have walls filled with colourful street art, graffiti, stencils and art installations. These art pieces range from the humorous to the counter-cultural. Visitors to this lane usually end up with a cocktail at Misty, a popular pre-theatre venue for theatre goers to the Forum Theatre.

There are other laneways that deserve mention. Cohen Place which is located between Russell Street and Exhibition street is noteworthy for a pair of marble lions at Cohen Place Plaza, a replica of a Ming dynasty archway (which donated by the Chinese government) and a bronze statue of Dr Sun Yat-Sen.

Hardware Lane, located between Elizabeth Street and Bourke Street, was named after Hardware House and sits on land formerly occupied by Kirk's Horse Bazaar, a horse and livery trading centre. Today it is a popular lane for bars and restaurants and tends to be a lively street at night.

Literature Lane is a bluestone-paved lane which is located midway along Little La Trobe Street. In May 2012 the Lord Mayor Robert Doyle used the lane to launch the National Year of Reading in recognition of Melbourne's 2008 status as a UNESCO City of Literature.

Windsor Place is located behind the Hotel Windsor and formerly known as Lang Lane. The Hotel Windsor was set up in 1883 by shipping magnate George Nipper as a luxury hotel. The lane was renamed after the hotel in 1943.

Dame Edna Place is a dead-end lane named in honour of much loved Melbourne icon and comedian, Barry Humphries, as the character Dame Edna Everage in 2007. Dame Edna's international reputation grew, putting Melbourne on the world map, and this was an effort to give

AC/DC Lane

her the recognition in her hometown. The lane is located off Little Collins Street, between Swanston and Elizabeth streets.

Degraves Street, located north of Flinders Street, is a popular lane both with tourists and locals for a coffee and a quick meal. You will notice the tables lined up in the centre of the lane in between shops on either side and protected by canopies and awnings. The lane is lively throughout the day with coffee drinkers.

GOINGS-ON

In any month of the year, you will find a festival, music, arts, a performance or a comedy to experience in Melbourne. Check out www.whatson.melbourne.vic.gov.au for a list of events.

A street artist at work

A Quick Snapshot

January	Australian Open Tennis
March	Formula 1 Grand Prix
March–April	Melbourne International Comedy Festival
June	Melbourne International Jazz Festival
July	Melbourne International Film Festival
August	Melbourne Writer's Festival
September	AFL Grand Final
October	Melbourne International Arts Festival
November	Melbourne Cup

Music Festivals

There is a music festival held every month in Melbourne and Victoria. The Melbourne International Jazz Festival held in June brings music from all over the world while the Melbourne International Singers Festival (also held in June) showcases choirs and singers. The Melbourne Music Week held in

Public Holidays

1 January	New Year's Day
26 January	Australia Day
2nd Monday in March	Labour Day
Variable date	Good Friday
Variable date	Easter Sunday
Variable date	Easter Monday
25 April	Anzac Day
2nd Monday in June	Queen's Birthday
Variable date	AFL Grand Final Day
1st Tuesday of November	Melbourne Cup Day
25 December	Christmas Day
26 December	Boxing Day

November in the CBD has hundreds of acts across town. For more details, see www.visitvictoria.com.au

The Melbourne International Arts Festival held in October is an international festival that showcases dance, theatre, music and performance art around the city.

SPORTS

Australia has a proud sporting tradition and there are numerous sports played in Melbourne, recognised as the nation's sporting capital. Melbourne hosted the Olympic Games in 1956 when Australian swimmer Dawn Fraser won the 100-m women's freestyle. In April 2016, the city received the ultimate accolade, being named Sports City of the Decade at the Ultimate Sports City awards in Switzerland, trumping Berlin, London, New York and Sydney. In a report on Melbourne as a Global Cultural Destination in 2017, the Boston Consulting Group affirms the city as Australia's cultural and sporting capital. There is a wide array of cultural and sporting events hosted in Melbourne throughout the year. Over 60 types of sports are played here. In football alone there are eight types of football played such as Australian Football League (AFL), Gaelic, Grid Iron, Rugby, Soccer and Touch Rugby.

There are sporting events held throughout the year with a dedicated rugby stadium, football stadium and tennis stadium. Whether or not you play a sport, you can enjoy being a spectator at the event. Melbourne is the place for world-class cricket (at the Ashes), Australian Rules Football, car racing (at the Formula 1 Grand Prix), motorcycle racing (at the Australian Motorcycle Grand Prix) and horse racing (at the Melbourne Cup).

AFL

The Australian Football League (AFL) which plays Australian Rules football is the most popular sport in Melbourne. The First played between two private schools in Melbourne in the 1950s, the game then had its own set of rules, balls and the length of the games differed. Under the Victorian Football Association, the rules evolved and the games became legalised in 1911 as Aussie Rules. The games turned fully professional in the 1990s. Although it was played initially only by teams in Victoria as the Victorian Football League, the sport was extended to other states and was renamed the Australian Football League in 1990. Among the popular teams are Carlton, Collingwood, Hawthorn and St Kilda.

The Friday preceding the Australian Football League Grand Final became a public holiday in Victoria in 2015, known as "AFL Grand Final Friday". Celebrated by families, it is an event that sees families of all ages dressed up and with faces painted in the colours of their favourite competing team.

AFL Sir Doug Nicholls Round

The AFL honours and celebrates indigenous players and culture each year through the Sir Doug Nicholls Round, formerly called AFL Indigenous Round. It is named for Sir Doug Nicholls, who played 54 games for Fitzroy, was the first Aboriginal person to be knighted and served as Governor of South Australia. There are only 155 players known to be of Aboriginal descent who have played AFL football. Fitzroy's Joe Johnson was the first known player of Aboriginal descent to play at AFL level. He played 55 games, including premierships in 1904 and 1905.

Rugby

Rugby Union and Rugby League are team sports derived from the UK, with some differences between them. Rugby Union has a more diverse group of players compared to Rugby League which is popular with boys from private schools. Rugby Union has 15 players while Rugby League has 13 players. The Rugby League has been professional since 1907-8 while the Rugby Union is played by amateurs.

AAMI Park Melbourne Rectangular Stadium is the venue for most rugby games in Melbourne. It has a seating capacity of 30,050 and gives all spectators a 180-degree view of the game. It is the home ground of Melbourne City Football Club (A-League), Melbourne Storm Rugby League Club (NRL) and the Melbourne Rebels (Super Rugby).

Cricket

Cricket is a religion in Melbourne. You need to know a little about the game even if you don't follow it closely. Unlike Australian rules football, which is played within the country, cricket is played internationally. It was introduced in the 1800s and competed nationally since the 1870s. The Australian test cricket team plays international matches yearly against

Britain, and other Commonwealth countries such as New Zealand, South Africa, India, Pakistan and the West Indies. The matches between England and Australia which are held every three to four years is known as "the Ashes", named after the burnt remains of a cricket ball used in a test match in 1882. There have been famous Australian cricketers, such as Sir Donald Bradman, a batsman in the 1930s and 1940s, and Shane Warne, one of the world's greatest leg spin bowlers in the late 1990s to the early 2000s.

At suburban parks you will find many Melburnians playing cricket in the weekend as the game is not only played on playing fields.

A ball tampering scandal involving the Australian cricket team in South Africa in March 2018 led to intense media scrutiny. Results of Cricket Australia's investigation placed the blame squarely on three players which included the captain, Steve Smith, and vice-captain, David Warner. They were suspended from the game for one year. The public outcry shows the level of integrity and professionalism Australians expect from their players. However, this does not diminish the love for cricket in Melbourne.

Tennis

Melbourne Park is a sports venue—comprising the Rod Laver Arena, Hisense Arena and Margaret Court Arena—that has hosted the Australian Open since 1988. Steffi Graf and Mats Wilander were the inaugural singles champions at the first match of the Australian Open. The centre court, which was previously known as Flinders Park or the National Tennis Centre, was renamed Rod Laver Arena in 2000, in recognition of the Australian player who achieved the Grand Slam twice. Basketball, netball and music concerts are also held here.

Swimming

In almost every suburb, the local council runs a sports centre with a gym and pool. These facilities offer an affordable venue for swimming but tend to be crowded during the weekends.

Ian Thorpe is a record setting freestyle swimmer and Australia's most successful Olympian with five gold, three silver and one bronze medal under his belt.

A match at the Australian Open

Motor Racing

Motor car enthusiasts in Melbourne enjoy the annual Australian Grand Prix held in Albert Park in Melbourne. This race has been held since 1928 at Phillip Island before the venue moved to Albert Park. Under a contract with Formula One, the Australian Grand Prix World Championship will be held until 2023. Road racing, drag racing and speedway races are held at other venues in Victoria such as Calder Park, Avalon Raceway and Sandown International Motor Raceway.

Hockey, Hurling and Roller Derby

Hockey is a popular sport for men and women in Melbourne. It is played recreationally and competitively. There is an international festival of hockey held in Melbourne in November since 2016 where teams from countries such as New Zealand, Netherlands, Japan, Pakistan and the United States compete.

Hurling is an outdoor team game of ancient Gaelic and Irish origin. It is played in Melbourne and resembles Gaelic football.

Roller derby first began in Chicago, USA in 1935 and is a team game of 14 players. What is popular today is the women's flat track roller derby. The Victorian All Stars became the first non-US team to be ranked number one in the world.

Winter Sports

During the winter months in June to August, skiing, ice skating and snowboarding are available. These sports have been popular since the 1860s when recreational skiing was developed. Australians have competed in the Winter Olympics since 1936.

Ice hockey has been a sport in Victoria since 1906 when a Victorian representative team and American sailors played at the Melbourne Glaciarium. Ice Hockey Australia is the official national governing body of ice hockey and a member of the International Ice Hockey Federation. Its beginnings can be traced back to 12 September 1908. Australia owns the oldest ice hockey trophy outside of North America called the Goodall Cup, which was first awarded on 4 September 1909. It is awarded to champions of the national hockey league, the Australian Ice Hockey League.

Skating

Melbourne has indoor ice rinks and there is an interstate short track speed skating competition run by the Australian Amateur Ice Racing Council.

Alpine Skiing

The state of Victoria has several well serviced resorts at Mount Buller, Falls Creek, Mount Hotham, Mount Baw Baw and Mount Buffalo where alpine skiing and cross country skiing are available. It is common for ski enthusiasts to drive for a weekend away at a resort to try out the slopes. These winter sports are not new as Australian skiers have competed in the Winter Olympics since 1952 in Oslo. For couch potatoes, there are many sports that may be followed on the television during winter.

HOBBIES

You can join a meet-up group for a hobby or an interest on www.meetup.com in Melbourne or you can even start your own hobby group. There are local community hobby groups which you can find on www.melbourne.vic.gov.au and www.eventbrite.com.au.

The Melbourne Cup

The Melbourne Cup, Australia's biggest horse racing event that draws both Australians and international visitors, is only celebrated in Melbourne and has been a public holiday there since 1877. Almost every Melburnian celebrates the "the race that stops a nation". Held on the first Tuesday of November at 3pm, it is customary to bet on a horse whether or not you know anything about racing. For ladies, it is a high fashion event where cocktail dresses and elegant hats are worn. For many it is an excuse to drink and get drunk.

There is an interesting story as to how this event's celebration changed from a dressy formal affair to a more carnival-like affair with a party vibe. In 1954, the model Jean Shrimpton came to the event in "The Shrimp's short skirt" that ended 10 cm above the knee, and without hat, gloves or stockings, much to Melbourne's outrage.

After his tour of Australia in 1895, Mark Twain wrote, "And so the grandstands make a brilliant and wonderful spectacle, a delirium of colour, a vision of beauty. The champagne flows, everybody is vivacious, excited, happy, everybody bets and gloves and fortunes change hands right along all the time … And at the end of the great week the swarms secure lodgings and transportation for next year then flock away to their remote homes and count their gains and losses, and order next year's Cup clothes, and then lie down and sleep two weeks, and get up sorry to reflect that a whole year must be put in somehow or other before they can be wholly happy again." (from *The Complete Travel Books, Anecdotes & Memoirs of Mark Twain*)

TRAVELLING AROUND AUSTRALIA

Australia, being a continent, is huge and travelling within the country can be costly.

Flying is the best option if you want to cover a large distance in a short time. However, domestic airfares can be costly despite the competition between a few airlines: Qantas, Virgin Australia, Tiger Airways and Jetstar. Booking in advance and checking for online deals may offer better prices.

Driving may be the best option if you have the time and flexibility to plan your journey. You can drive a car, a four wheel drive, a motorhome, motorbike or caravan. The choice is yours depending on your budget.

Many grey nomads (retirees) have hit the road travelling at leisure in a motorhome or caravan. You can choose to buy or hire your motorhome or caravan. They are comfortable and a cheaper option to a motel or hotel. A night's stay at a caravan park costs between A$30 to A$60 per night, cheaper than most motels and hotels. A common choice for many is travelling on a Toyota Landcruiser or Nissan Patrol towing a caravan or motorhome. This is a snapshot of things to consider if you go down this route:

Always carry enough **water, food and supplies**. Buy food at supermarkets in the city before you head to the bush (rural areas). Supplies like groceries and toiletries may be more expensive in the bush. It is recommended that you carry at least four to five litres of water a day, per person.

You cannot pack everything you need for a long trip so pack the basics. You would need to shop every few days for the extras. Fresh food and perishables will rot unless consumed so store more canned and dried foods and freeze meats for the journey. As space is limited a one pot is recommended such as an all-in-one pot or a slow cooker.

Petrol costs tend to be higher in the bush. You can use apps like Motormouth, FuelCheck and GasBuddy to check fuel prices.

It is recommended that you stock up with a battery and a generator for **power** sources, depending on the length of your journey.

Most Australians travel up to the Northern Territory during **winter** to avoid the cold. Avoid December to March because of the wet season and the risk of flash floods. Tasmania offers a slightly cooler **summer** so many travel there in summer.

Traveling with **pets** is restrictive as not all places are pet friendly. National parks and caravan parks do not allow pets.

Always check the details of your **insurance** policy. Some policies do not cover driving on unsealed roads.

Always be prepared for the **weather**. Bring sunscreen, hats, insect repellents for protection.

When travelling into the bush, be warned that mobile phone coverage even with 4G can be limited if not non-existent. Options for **communications** are a portable broadband dongle, satellite Wi-Fi and portable Wi-Fi router.

Prepare your **children** for the road by equipping them with a map and the planned route so that they are more aware of the long road ahead. Fill the motorhome with familiar items such as pillows, stuffed toys and books, to make the environment more comfortable for them. Follow a routine with the children. Although this may seem like an extended holiday, keeping to a fixed bedtime will make things easier.

Plan the **entertainment** for the journey by downloading games and videos on an iPad. A few favourite board games would also be handy. Stop at parks or playgrounds along the way. This will relieve the monotony of a long journey which may be up to 350 km a day and give everyone a chance to breathe some fresh air and move around. Keep a card with your details and mobile numbers in your children's pockets, in case they get lost.

Safety

When travelling around Australia, be aware of the risks posed by wildlife, such as snakes and spiders. Everyone needs to be prepared to stop, freeze and move backwards to safety if they see a snake. If you are travelling north, be prepared for crocodiles in the water and know how to deal with them.

As most vehicles do not observe the speed limits and rules in a caravan park ("Drive at walking pace"), you should advise children to walk with care. If you are walking with your children, be on the lookout for fast moving vehicles.

Other Travel Options

Travelling by coach is another option. Greyhound, Australia's national coach operator offers popular routes and flexible passes depending on the length of your journey. Firefly Express operates from Melbourne, Adelaide and Sydney.

Travelling by train is an option which offers comfort and you can leave the stress of driving behind you. It is not cheap but you can enjoy the beautiful scenery. The Indian Pacific links Sydney, Adelaide and Perth in three days, crossing the great Nullarbor Plain in the process; the Ghan from Adelaide takes you to the Red Centre, Alice Springs; Darwin XPT trains link Sydney with Melbourne and Brisbane at affordable prices; and Queensland Railways links Brisbane with Townsville and Cairns. For more information, visit www.australian-trains.com.

There are cruiselines and freightliners which offer travel by sea to Australian cities. Popular ones are P&O cruises and Spirit of Tasmania.

New Zealand is regarded as the top travel destinations for Australian tourists, as it is just a hop and a jump away or a "hop across the pond". Touring, skiing, cycling, golf and business events are some of the reasons Australians like to visit their neighbour. Bali is another favourite for Melburnians, who seek warm beaches, sea activities, cheap food and beer and the sun to escape the cold winters in Melbourne.

WEEKEND NOTES

There is a plethora of choices on offer on how to spend weekends. Take a walk, hike or picnic at the many parks in Melbourne. On a sunny day, vintage cars driving along the freeways make for a captivating sight. Beaches are crowded with families enjoying the good weather. During winter, it is common for many to go skiing at the mountains to enjoy the snow. My husband's colleague took a ride on a steam engine for the weekend. The possibilities are endless.

PLACES OF INTEREST
State Library of Victoria

The State Library of Victoria was established in 1854 as the Melbourne Public Library and is the state's premier reference and research library. It also provides museum and gallery space. Entrance to the library is free and the collection includes historical documents like John Batman's journal, old armour pieces of famous bushranger and outlaw Ned Kelly, and paintings such as William Strutt's *Black Thursday, February 6th, 1851*. Every year, more than 70,000 items are added to the collection.

The La Trobe Reading Room is home to heritage furniture made from native timber, and a famed concrete dome which allows in natural light. The Mirror of the World exhibition on the fourth floor showcases books including a 4,000-year-old Sumerian cuneiform tax receipt and very old religious texts.

The Royal Botanic Gardens Victoria

This park in the city spans 38 ha. Visitors can choose to experience the Aboriginal Heritage Walk, the Garden Discovery Tour, a ride on the Garden Explorer, or tour the Children's Garden. Entrance is free and a visitor has many options besides the walks, to sit and read a book, enjoy a tea in a café, or take a ride on the pond. There are the outdoor cinema, theatre performances and exhibitions which are enjoyed in the warmer months. There is also a Melbourne Observatory tour of the night sky.

Federation Square

This building with its patterned cobblestones from the Kimberley region in Western Australia, and clad with fractal-patterned reptilian skin is a focus point for many visitors and locals. It is located opposite Flinders Street Station. The site has bars and exhibition spaces, and is home to the Australian Centre for the Moving Image, and the Ian Potter Centre, NGV Australia, which showcases Australian art. The outdoor offers spaces to sit and enjoy the view of the Yarra and outdoor performances.

Arts Centre Melbourne

This is Melbourne's leading venue for world-class theatre, dance and music. In the Theatres Building are three separate theatres—the State Theatre (which boasts one of the world's largest stages and hosts performances by Opera Australia and The Australian Ballet), the Playhouse and the intimate Fairfax Studio. Hamer Hall is next door and is a premier venue for musical performances, including the Melbourne Symphony Orchestra. There are daily guided tours, free exhibitions and a Sunday market. The Australian

Federation Square

Music Vault features a free exhibition celebrating Australian contemporary music.

St Kilda

This is Melbourne's version of the New Jersey boardwalk. The neighbourhood offers an arts scene, food, a walk on the beach and pier, a chance to spot penguins and enjoy an old-fashioned family theme park, Luna Park, with the Scenic Railway roller coaster that started operations in 1912. The latter also offers stunning views of Port Phillip Bay. At night, the area buzzes with music venues, pubs and restaurants.

Sculptural work, *Early Morning Coffee,* at St Kilda

Phillip Island

A popular choice for families, photographers and nature lovers, the main attraction has always been the penguins with a "Little Penguin Parade" at dusk as the colony returns to land for the evening. Visitors can enjoy eco tours, guided ranger talks, koala sightings, and the relaxed environment away from the city. There are also markets, restaurants, spas and boutique shops.

Phillip Island is also the site for mutton birds. Since 1880s, tourists have flocked to sight these birds. Also known as short tailed shearwaters, these birds migrated from Alaska to Phillip Island for breeding, leaving their eggs in burrows.

Eureka Tower

This is a 297-m tall skyscraper located in the Southbank precinct which allows visitors to enjoy a complete 360 degree, floor-to-ceiling view of Melbourne's CBD, sports precinct, the Docklands and everything in between. It was completed on 1 June 2006 and named after the Eureka Rebellion in Ballarat, Victoria in 1854. The tower houses the 88-level Eureka Skydeck 88, a uniquely shaped blue-glass structure. There is also the enclosed all-glass cube, known as the Edge, which extends 3 m (9.84 ft) out from the viewing platform, where a visitor can stand "suspended" over the city on a clear glass floor.

The Shrine of Remembrance

This magnificent memorial to Victorians killed in World War I was built between 1928 and 1934, its classical design partly based on the Mausoleum of Halicarnassus, one of the seven ancient wonders of the world. The shrine's upper balcony gives visitors an unobstructed view of the Melbourne skyline, all the way up to Swanston Street.

The shrine is the site for the annual Anzac Day dawn service. The Remembrance Day service held on 11 November commemorates the signing of the 1918 Armistice which marked the end to WWI. At 11am, a shaft of light shines through an opening in the ceiling, passing over the Stone of Remembrance and illuminating the word "love". The Galleries of Remembrance located below the shrine has a museum with 800 historical artefacts and artworks on Australians at war.

The Great Ocean Road

This scenic drive along Victoria's coast allows visitors to enjoy the breath-taking ocean views with magnificent surfs, seaside towns, limestone cliffs dairy farms and heathlands. There are many beaches to be enjoyed, and lighthouses and forests to visit. The road stretches for 243 km along winding curves. The famous 12 Apostles, limestone monoliths protruding from the sea, have been eroded with time and currently there are only eight Apostles left.

The Yarra Valley

This is the perfect area to enjoy Victorian wine and the opportunity for a weekend retreat. Located within the Yarra Ranges National Park, it spans from Healesville, Warburton to Williamstown in Port Philip Bay. The valley boasts more than 80 wineries, restaurants, national parks and wildlife. Visitors can go winery hopping, enjoy a relaxing weekend away or rise at dawn to take in the sights from a hot air balloon over the valley.

The Dandenong Ranges

This is the perfect place to get in touch with nature. Located only an hour away from the city, it is home to many attractions such as the Dandenong Ranges Botanic Garden (formerly the National Rhododendron Garden) with its colourful array of flowers such as rhododendrons, camellias and azaleas, villages such as Gembook, Kallista, quaint eateries such as Miss Marples Tea Room for an afternoon tea of scones, and Sky High Mount Dandenong which has cafes and a restaurant with a panoramic view of the city.

The Mornington Peninsula

Covering the land between Port Phillip Bay and Western Port Bay, the peninsula is home to many attractions such as

The Great Ocean Road

Arthurs Seat, Point Nepean National Park and towns such as Sorrento and Mornington. The region has been a popular tourist spot since the 1870s. There are many attractions to explore such as art galleries, golf courses, adventure gardens, beautiful landscapes, sea sports such as diving and fishing, and swimming with dolphins.

It is also a popular area for vineyards and gourmet food where you can linger over a lunch or dinner at a winery while enjoying the scenery. There are more than 50 wineries to choose from.

The Cape Schanck Light station which was built in 1859 is a limestone lighthouse located on the peninsula's remote southwest tip. Arthur's Seat is another attraction with its modern chairlift in the style of a Swiss-built gondola, where you can sit and enjoy panoramic views spanning Melbourne's city skyline to the Madecon ranges.

The Peninsula Hot Springs is a favourite for Melburnians and best enjoyed in the cooler months. These geothermal hot springs offer special deals throughout the year. There are also many spas where you can enjoy a massage. It is located just an hour's drive from the south of Melbourne.

Daylesford and the Macedon Ranges

Daylesford is a town where visitors can spend a weekend of fresh country air, natural mineral springs, good produce and good wine. Located at the bottom of the Great Dividing Range of Victoria, one can enjoy walks at the Wombat Hill Botanical Gardens which is on top of an extinct volcano, or the Hepburn Regional Park for its flora and fauna. For those who wish to do more than eating and relaxing, there is golf, fishing, and bush walking.

The dormant volcano at Hanging Rock is the scene for mystery and adventure. The story behind Hanging Rock, made famous by the classic novel, *Picnic at Hanging Rock,* by Joan Lindsay and adapted into the 1975 movie by Peter Weir, tells of a Valentine's Day disappearance of a group of schoolgirls and their teacher while visiting Hanging Rock in 1901.

CHAPTER 8

AUSTRALIAN ENGLISH

STREWTH! MATE!!!

AUSLANG ENGLISH

TRIGG.

> **❝**More languages are spoken in Melbourne than there are countries in the world, a cacophony of 251 tongues whose voices stretch to all corners of the city.**❞**

— *The Age*, 11 July 2017

PECULIARITIES

Even as early as the 1890s, Australian English was already recognised as being different from English spoken in England or Americas. It has been reported that it was Mark Twain who on a visit to Australia in 1897 noticed a tendency for Australians to flatten certain vowels in their speech. In 1912, Sidney Baker published *The Australian Language,* the first study on written and spoken English in Australia. Academic interest on Australian English developed from the 1960s.

Early Australian English developed based on the social class of the early immigrants: English settlers who came with their Cockney accent. From the early settlers, we get the

word "swag", whose meaning has changed from a bundle of stolen goods to its present day meaning, a sleeping bag. The language has also been influenced by the Aboriginals who contributed vocabulary such as "koala" and "kangaroo" to the language and the adoption of Aboriginal names and words such as "billabong" and "Canberra". "Billabong" refers to a dead river or an oxbow lake or an isolated pond left behind after a river changes course. Canberra, the capital of Australia means "meeting place" in the local Ngunnawal language. With growing nationalism, Australian English has taken a life of its own and the Macquarie Dictionary and the Australian National Dictionary attest to its status.

In his book, *The Story of Australian English*, Kel Richards, an Australian author, explains that Aussie English consists of four different components: slangs, non-slang vocabulary, accent and grammar. By the term slang, it refers to language which differs from standard or written speech in vocabulary or construction. Non-slang vocabulary refers to words unique to Australia. For example, a flat in London is referred to as an apartment in New York, a condo in Singapore and a unit in Australia. "Damper" is a term only used in Australia to refer to bread made in a camp oven while in the bush. The grammar is a mix of morphology and syntax. For example, it is common for Aussies to add the phrase "Wahddaya reckon?" when they wish to say, "Is that so?" Aussie English has morphed to include diminutives and this is prevalent in conversational English in Melbourne.

A few words in Aussie English today come from British regional dialects from the first settlers. These include the words "billy", "dinkum", "bloke" and "sheila". "Billy", referring to a pot to boil water usually used at a campside, is derived from a Scottish dialect. "Dinkum", which means work, derives from the miners in Derbyshire. "Bloke" and "sheila" are Aussie words for a guy and a girl.

Aboriginal words that are part of the language today include "jarrah", "jackaroo", "wallaby", "wombat" and "yakka". "Jarrah" refers to a tall tree found in Western Australia while a jackaroo is a young man who works on a sheep or cattle stations. The words "wallaby" and "wombat" are Aboriginal Dharuk words which mean a small kangaroo and a marsupial respectively. "Yakka" means hard work.

Andrew Barton Paterson, an Australian author more popularly known as Banjo Paterson, was one of Australia's most famous poets. Paterson is the author of the bush ballad *The Man from Snowy River* and the Australian folk song *Waltzing Matilda*. A lot of his work involved the use and promotion of Aussie slang. The term "mate" was used by Paterson in his poem *Clancy of the Overflow* and the expression "jumbuck" was used in *Waltzing Matilda*.

Most people associate Australia with the phrase "no worries". It seems fitting as it is a relaxed way of saying all is well, or no problems. While the exact origins of the phrase is not known, the use of this phrase is now global and part of everyday spoken English.

Gone are the days when English was the only language spoken in Melbourne. The influx of migrants over the years has led to many different tongues being spoken. According to a study in 2016, Mandarin is the most spoken language other than English in homes in Melbourne today. In Greater Melbourne, the proportion of those who speak English is only 62 per cent of the population; 32 per cent speak a non-English language. For those who speak English and wish to become assimilated with Melbourne society, there is some learning to do in order to speak Aussie English. So how easy is it for a foreigner to pick up English in Melbourne and is Australian English different from British English? Australian English, or Strine as it called, is what differentiates English spoken in Australia from that spoken in America or the United Kingdom.

There are a few features in Aussie English that you need to be aware of—the use of diminutives, idioms and abbreviations in spoken English.

Australian Women Writers

Nancy Keesing was born in 1923 in Sydney and contributed to the growth of Australian slang. She was an Australian author and poet whose work as a prolific writer involved the study of the domestic use of Aussie English by Australian women and families. In her book, *Lily on the Dustbin*, she reveals a specific type of Australian slang, calling it Sheilaspeak or Familyspeak. The expression "Lily on the Dustbin" refers to a woman dressed ostentatiously at a social event or a woman who is isolated at a social event.

June Factor wrote about the contribution by Australian children to the language. In her book *Kidspeak: A Dictionary of Australian Children's Words, Expressions and Games* (2000), she shows that Australian children are verbal inventors of words, similar to how Australians have created their own slang over the years. Among the words invented as "braceface" which is an insulting term for a person who wears dental braces and "brinnie", which refers to a small stone used by school boys to throw at each other in the school yard.

Source: *The Story of Australian English* by Kel Richards (New South Publishing, 2015)

DIMINUTIVES

Aussies are fond of shortening their words. The term "Aussie" was born in the First World War and was described in the Australian National Dictionary as referring to the country not the person. However by the 1920s, the use of the word which referred to the people as well as the country became mainstream. The use of diminutives which is shortening a word or phrase makes the word sound less pretentious and more friendly. Examples of such expressions are "arvo" for afternoon, "avo" for avocado, "tradie" for a tradesperson, "truckie" for truck driver, "Macca" for McDonalds, and "cuppa" for a cup of tea.

ABBREVIATIONS

Aussies also like to use abbreviations in their language. Perhaps they believe that being informal makes them more friendly. Interestingly, Aussies do not refer to their country in full as a visitor would, but call it "Straya". And how do they pronounce it? They tend to drag the syllables and it sounds like "Straaayah". The national carrier, QANTAS, also is also an abbreviation of Queensland and Northern Territory Airline Service.

IDIOMS

There are many idioms that Australians use but some are more commonplace. The best way a newcomer could familiarise themselves is to look at websites or books. Here's a sampling:

Bludger: a person who is lazy or doesn't work
Bloody ripper: really awesome
Fair dinkum: an exclamation saying something is true or genuine
Fair suck of the sauce bottle: an Aussie slang used by ex-Prime Minister Kevin Rudd to mean a fair treatment. It was understood by struggling Aussie families who had to share

tomato sauce with family members to flavour their meat. It is similar to "having a fair go" or a "fair crack of the whip".

Nah, yeah: Yes

Sausage sizzle: a sausage served in white bread with tomato sauce. A common sight in the weekends outside Bunnings or supermarkets; proceeds are used to raise funds by educational or social groups

She'll be right: Everything will be fine

Shout: to buy the next round of drinks

Stubby: a can of beer

True blue: genuine; authentically Australian

Turps: alcohol

Yeah, nah: No.

A list of common Aussie expressions can be found at the end of this chapter.

PROFANITY AND INFORMALITY

The use of profanity is Aussie English is well known. An off cited Australian saying goes, "If the guy next to you is swearing like a wharfie, there is a good chance he may be a billionaire or perhaps just a wharfie." This shows that the use of swear words is not limited to a type of person but shared

by Australians from all walks of life. Politicians have used it to show a kinship with Aussies of all classes.

The infamous Tourism Australia clip which used the word "bloody" in 2006 was an A$180 million advertising campaign. The advertisement showed Australians preparing for visitors to their country, followed by partygoers at the harbour watching fireworks, ending with a bikini-clad model stepping out of the water asking, "So where the bloody hell are you?"

The advertisement was banned in the United Kingdom for the use of the word "bloody". When an Aussie asks, "Where the bloody hell are ya?", you may feel offended but the average Australian may not react negatively or treat this as an insult. It is merely their way of asking, "Where are you?"

The use of swear words has infiltrated surprising circles. The Minister for Immigration and Border Protection Peter Dutton once called a journalist a "mad f---ing witch", and Senator David Leyonhjelm called a fellow Twitter user a "c---". Former Prime Minister Kevin Rudd has been recorded using the f-word. Not quite what a conversative newcomer or migrant to Australia may be used to!

Bernard, an Austrian, found himself surprised by the informality of language in Melbourne. Walking into Maccas,

he was greeted by a friendly waiter who asked him, "How you goin', mate? What would you like today?" Bernard had forgotten how informal Australians could be and felt uncomfortable being called "mate" as he was used to the formality of being addressed as "Sir" while in Europe.

Another friend, Sarah, an Asian teacher who had taught primary school students in Malaysia, was used to being addressed with respect by the students as "Mrs Lee". Teaching in Melbourne, she had to get used to being addressed by eight year olds as "Sarah". Whether at the office or other workplaces, you would find that no matter how senior the person you are speaking to is, you can call that person by his or her first name.

SPELLING AND GRAMMAR

Australia uses a mix of American and British in the spelling of words. You will notice this on certain advertising material. For example, The Australian Labor Party adopted the American spelling of "labor" in the early 20th century in order to associate itself with American libertarian ideals. Certain words like "programme" and "organisations" have been seen spelt American style as "program" and "organization". Educational institutions such as Melbourne University and Monash University, however, do follow the British spelling and their teachers do stress this distinction.

The view that Australian grammar is a mix of British and American English was raised by a young Australian, Gemma Sapwell, a radio and TV producer who's worked at the ABC, and who went to school in the 1980s and 1990s. She lamented the lack of formal grammar education in Australia due to the liberal "whole language" approach, rather than traditional drill methods. She says she made it through the entire education system without being taught how to properly structure a sentence.

THE AUSTRALIAN ACCENT

According to many linguists, the origins of the Australian accent evolved from a process called levelling down. The early settlers from England were people with different dialects and who spoke differently and therefore had to "level" their dialect to be understood by each other. There are humourous alternative theories behind the accent which suggest that pollen levels may have contributed to the nasal twang, or even that Aussies started mumbling to stop flies from entering into their mouths! By the 20th century, there were three distinct accents in Australia: a general Australian accent, a cultivated British-sounding accent and a very broad "ocker" (uncultivated) accent.

A broad accent, used by the late Steve Irwin or Kath and Kim, is associated with a more "bogan" (country or unsophisticated) type accent. A cultivated accent sounds more like an English accent—listen to Cate Blanchett or Geoffrey Rush. A general accent is in between the bogan and cultivated accents—Hugh Jackman is a good example.

There is no set accent for a Melburnian and it would depend on who you socialise with or where you studied and your social class.

Linguists from the University of Melbourne have reported that you can identify a Melburnian by asking them where they are from. According to a report on SBS World News Online, Melburnians were likely to respond by saying "Malbourne". Dr Debbie Loake has found a specific sound change evident in speakers from Melbourne and Southern Victoria, where "el" sounds are becoming confused with "al" sounds.

EXPRESSIONS

The use of words and expressions differ from state to state. Here are some differences:

General term	Melbourne	Sydney	Other states
swimwear	bathers/ togs	swimmers	togs (Queensland)
potato cakes	potato cakes	potato scallops	potato fritter (Western Australia)
sausage on a slice of bread	sausage in bread	sausage sandwich or sanger	

There are other expressions that Aussies use which you can only understand once you are in Australia. Some of the expressions and their meanings are:

All over it like a seagull on a sick prawn	A crowd that gathers around someone/something
All over the place like a wet dog on lino	Confusion or disorder
Ave a go, ya mug	Have a go at it; try harder
Better than a poke in the eye with a burnt stick	Things are not that bad

Cheeky little possum	An incorrigible but endearing child
Chuck a wobbly	Throw a tantrum; lose one's temper
Dry as ... a dead dingo's donga	Very thirsty
Flat out like a lizard drinking	Very busy
Frog in a sock	Very successful; losing your temper
Game as Ned	Foolishly brave
Get a Guernsey	Selected for a sports team or line up
Happy little Vegemites	Happy children
Lower than a snake's belly	Untrustworthy
Missed it by a bee's dick	A narrow miss
She's apples	Everything's fine
Wouldn't shout in a shark attack	Someone who is hesitant to buy someone a beer
You beaut!	You're a champion or winner

LEARNING DIFFICULTIES FOR FOREIGNERS

I learnt a few Aussie expressions while doing renovations to my house. I learnt about "tradies", tradesperson with skills such as carpenters and plumbers. I also worked with a "sparky", an electrician who does the wiring for electricity.

When ordering a burger, you may notice that Aussie may order one with "the lot", meaning an Aussie burger containing meat, lettuce, egg, bacon, pineapple, cheese, beetroot and sauce. In fact the addition of beetroot is an Aussie creation.

Going to the beach, you would find most people either

go barefoot or go with "thongs". This term does not refer to underwear but the ubiquitous rubber slippers or flip flops.

Soccer is not to be confused with "footy". Soccer refers to the English version of football with a round ball. Footy is rugby in its various forms such as Rugby Union, Rugby League, AFL and Touch football. In Melbourne, home to Australian Football Rules, footy is a term you need to know and be familiar with if you want to fit into society.

"No worries, mate" is a slang that is used not only in Melbourne and Australia, but an Australian contribution to the dictionary. Instead of the traditional, "You're welcome", this expression is how Aussies reply to "Thank you". It has become so popular that it is used worldwide. It can even be used in response to a request.

The word "bogan" is used to refer to an unsophisticated person who has little knowledge or understanding of the world. Such a person is likely to be a beer drinker or someone who is not fashionable. There was a television series by ABC called *Upper Middle Bogan*.

A typical Aussie conversation could go:

Bob: G'day mate!
John: G'day.
Bob: Would ya like to pop around for a cuppa?
John: Sure, mate. See ya in ten.
Bob: Actually, fancy a tinny instead?
John: Defo.

Translated, this conversation goes:

Bob: Good day, friend!
John: Good day.
Bob: Would you like to come over for a cup of tea?
John: Sure. I will see you in ten minutes.

Bob: Actually, would you like a can of beer instead?
John: Definitely.

It will take some time to get accustomed to Australian in slang and expressions. Enjoy the journey to becoming true blue!

IMPORTANCE OF ENGLISH

Henry, a European Australian, recalled that forty years ago, Australians were not yet used to people talking in foreign languages. He had an experience when he was told off in rude terms for talking, in a low voice, to his brother in Hungarian while on a tram. As he was a new migrant and was still learning English, he felt more comfortable speaking to his family in their language. Naturally he was upset. Today in Melbourne, you can hear quite a few different languages spoken in the city without eyebrows raised. As a Malaysian friend put it, most Australians are polite and tolerant and would not openly criticise foreigners speaking their own language. However by speaking English, you are able to fit into this cosmopolitan city. As he put it, it was mostly a language issue rather than a racial issue.

New migrants from non-English-speaking countries may encounter problems learning the language as they build a new life. An inability to express oneself is often traumatic and can make people feel lost, confused, even depressed.

Abdi Aden, a former refugee from Somalia, arrived in Australia in 1993 unable to speak English. Today he is a successful author and conducts workshops at the Melbourne Writers Festival. His book *Shining: The Story of a Lucky Man* was shortlisted for the NSW Premier's Literary Award in 2016. He explained in an interview with Royal Automobile Club of Victoria (RACV) magazine that he learnt English through attending cultural and social events. For his work as a youth worker, he was awarded the 2007 Victorian Refugee Recognition Award.

The Australian Government funds the Adult Migrant English Program. Eligible migrants and humanitarian entrants who speak little or no English are provided up to 510 hours of free English language tuition. AMES Australia helps new and recent refugees and migrants to settle into Victoria, and provides English classes. Its CEO Catherine Scarth has said that language was often the key to securing other essential aspects of life, including work, housing and a sense of social inclusion. To understand the language, there are Australian English dictionaries including the Australian Oxford Dictionary.

NON-VERBAL COMMUNICATION

Australians are known for being direct and this applies in Melbourne. Like most Western cultures, maintaining eye contact is important as it shows you are trustworthy. When you are trying to make a point, gesticulating or touching someone on the shoulder or arm is acceptable provided you know the person. Interestingly giving a thumbs up which would ordinarily be acceptable in other cultures, was not well received several years ago and was regarded as rude, but this is no longer the case.

When greeting a person, a firm, friendly handshake with a warm smile is a positive gesture. While you see many people, both male and female, greeting each other with a hug and a kiss, some men prefer a quick pat on the back.

Little most Western cultures, Melburnians are mindful of their personal space and it would be respectful to maintain an arm's length between you and the person standing next to you or even when you are face to face with another person. Melburnians are quite respectful of others and queue when in front of a cashier or otherwise. It is not good manners to cut queue, jump into line or barge in.

Traffic in Melbourne has increased and you will find that some drivers may appear aggressive when parking. Most times, drivers are courteous but occasionally, like anywhere else in the world, you can find a bad apple who is tailgating you, waiting dangerously too near to you for your spot as you reverse out of your lot, or angry drivers gesticulating and horning at you.

TELLING TIME

Many people who were new to Melbourne have cited their experience of being invited to "tea". Most thought the invitation was for afternoon tea but soon found out that it was an invitation to dinner instead. To many Melburnians, the reference to tea actually means dinner.

When it comes to telling the time, if you are from outside Australia, you would need to be familiar with expressions such as "Thursday week". If someone asks you to meet them Thursday week, what they mean is that they wish to meet you the following week on a Thursday.

While it may be common for some to arrange a meeting at 11:30am tomorrow, what you would commonly hear is the meeting will be at "half eleven". While you may be used to telling the time precisely as 5:15pm or 5:30am, an Aussie may say "fifteen past five in the evening" or "a quarter past five in the evening" or "a half five in the morning" instead.

It will take time to learn the language but have fun!

SOME AUSSIE SLANGS

Ace: Excellent

Akubra: A wide brimmed hat made of rabbit fur

Barbie: barbeque

Barrack: Support

Bottle-O: bottle shop, liquor store

Bloody: Very

Brickie: Bricklayer

Buckley's chance: Unlikely chance

Budgie smuggler: Speedo style bathing suits for men

Bung: Injured

Cactus: Not working

Chippie: Carpenter

Chockers: very full

Chunder: Vomit

Crikey: Expressing mild surprise

Dag: Socially awkward person

Daks: Trousers

Dingo's breakfast: No breakfast

Dinkum or **fair dinkum**: true, real, genuine

Drum: latest information or news

Dunny: Toilet

Esky: cooler

Furphy: rumour

Garbo: garbage collector

Grey nomads: Retirees that travel around Australia by car

Goon: cask wine

Hoon: Hooligan

Knock: To criticise

Moo juice: milk

Nanna: grandmother

Nature strip: the strip of grass planted between a footpath and a road

Mozzie: mosquito

Op shop: Opportunity shop or thrift store

Outlaws: In-laws

Pig's arse!: Not agreeing

Pash: Passionate kiss

Pav: Pavlova

Polly: Politician

Plonk: Cheap wine

Pos Smoko: Cigarette or coffee break

Quandong: A conman; a native fruit

Ripper: something wonderful or admirable

Rego: Car Registration

Root: Sexual intercourse

Rort: Scam or cheat

Rust-bucket: a car or something old and in a bad condition

RSL: Returned and Services League club

Sanger: Sandwich

Shout: your turn to pay or treat someone

Stoked: Pleased or delighted

Servo: Service station

Sunnies: Sunglasses

Sook: Whinger or to sulk

Sickie: sick day

Slab: 24-pack of beer

Schooner: Glass of beer

Strewth: Expressing shock or surprise

Ta: thank you

Tool: Idiotic person

Tucker: Food

Ute: Utility vehicle, pickup truck

U-ey: Making a u-turn

Veg out: Relax

Wag: Playing truant

Whinge: whine or complain

Wanker: An insulting and abusive term for a person

Wowser: A prude

CHAPTER 9

WORKING IN MELBOURNE

> ❝People call Australia the lucky country; but good fortune is an illusion without effort.❞

— Rupert Murdoch AC KCSG, Annual Lowry Institute Lecture: 2013 Address

YOUR FIRST JOB

Getting your first job in Melbourne is a big hurdle for most migrants. The Australians insist on Australian experience before they consider you for a position. Never mind that you have a PhD from Harvard or Oxford and have worked in many great cities. Invariably you will have to cut your teeth in Melbourne.

Changes to the world economy demand that Australia enters the information age. Migrants who settle well are usually highly skilled IT professionals, medical practitioners, and accountants. Highly skilled electricians and nurses are also in demand. Those who are hard hit by this change are labourers and factory workers; the reality of unemployment or underemployment has resulted in a growing number of Australians living below the poverty line. In the heart of the city of Melbourne, it is common to see homeless people on the streets. In 2018, there were at least 23,000 Victorians who were homeless.

The picture is not totally bleak. Once you get your first job and gather sufficient Australian experience, the doors will open for you to start your career in Melbourne. Although finding full-time employment is challenging, there are short-term employment opportunities available in Melbourne. For example, there are more jobs in the hospitality industry during the summer months. As Melbourne hosts lots of international events and festivals, there are always temporary jobs available.

The best way to secure employment is to register with human resource agencies, check employment websites, look at the Saturday editions of Melbourne newspapers, or look on online sites such as adzuna.com.au, seek.com.au and careerone.com.au.

As Melbourne is highly regulated, you should ensure that you have the appropriate certification for skilled work such as teaching, construction and hospitality. You should have an up-to-date resume with your contact details and suitable references. Once you have found a job, you will need to open a bank account and obtain a Tax File Number (TFN) from the Australian Taxation Office. For those without a Tax File Number, you may apply for one by visiting the post office to obtain an application form.

DRESS CODES

At the corporate workplace, most people dress formally and conservatively, choosing black as their main colour. Men wear dark suits, shirts and ties while women wear either skirts or trousers. Fridays are usually casual and most people dress down to smart casual attire. However there are still standards to abide by and jeans, shorts, and flip flops are not allowed. In the suburbs or outside the city centre, the dress code is more relaxed and would depend on the specific industry you work in.

The banking, finance and legal industries are the most conservative. For women, heavy jewellery and accessories may appear too flashy. If you are in a creative industry like the arts or advertising, there is more room to wear other colours. People tend to dress according to the season so during the hot summers, the business jacket may be removed.

THE WORKPLACE ENVIRONMENT

Most Australians in an office are punctual and abide by a professional work ethic. The normal working hours are 9am to 5:30pm (with an hour's lunch break) and most people would abide by these hours unless they are working part-time or overtime. In today's competitive world, many work overtime to meet deadlines. Although Australians may appear laid back, they tend to have good time management at work and absenteeism is frowned upon. You would need to work cooperatively and effectively with colleagues to meet your goals. Australians tend to observe how a new worker fits into the culture in the office. Take your time to smile and be friendly but observe the work culture before you say too much.

Australians are informal and usually go by a first name basis even at work. Given the egalitarian bent in the society, managers do not openly pull rank on their workers or lord over their staff. They tend to communicate effectively to their workers and guide them in their responsibilities. Managers adopt a pragmatic approach at the workplace and set boundaries. Do not be afraid of expressing your views and opinions as these will be taken into consideration.

Communication between management and staff at the workplace may at times appear combative or confrontational to the outsider. Being direct, Australians may seem to often debate with each other, but this is part of the collaborative culture. Managers usually make the final decision but there is room for consultation along the way. Obtaining the opinion of junior staff opens communication lines and helps improve workplace efficiencies.

Australians believe that there is dignity in labour. Whether the person is a shop assistant, chef, waitress or electrician, they are knowledgeable and their service standards are high. This explains the relatively high hourly rate that these workers are paid. If you are coming from a less developed country, you need to be mindful that they are not workers to be exploited at your beck and call but professionals.

During the course of my house renovations, I have learnt that true blue Aussies are punctual and professional. Workers arrived at my house at 7am in the morning and kept their breaks to a minimum. I was pleasantly surprised by the level of professionalism in their workmanship and how they always cleaned up after they have completed their work. This was quite unlike my experience in some parts of Asia.

SOCIALISING WITH COLLEAGUES AND CLIENTS

In certain cultures, before you enter into a business arrangement with the other party, you would have to wine and dine them in order to get their business. Australians, however, are direct in their business approach and you would not need to go out of your way to develop a personal relationship prior to working together. However, it's always good to start a meeting with some casual conversation. Melburnians like to know a little about your background and you can share where you went to school and your family to get the conversation going. Talking about sport is another conversation starter in Melbourne as the city is Australia's sporting capital.

When attending business meetings, timeliness and efficiency are paramount. You need to be honest in your communication rather than try to impress with ideas. Melburnians value your ability to complete the task rather than offer empty promises. Being concise and to the point will help. If you find that your views are being challenged in a meeting, do not take this personally. Australians like to debate over issues and this may escalate.

There is a sense of camaraderie among colleagues in the office and work colleagues do socialise after work over drinks. They exchange greetings in the mornings, asking about each other's weekends or plans for the week. This helps build up a friendly and open workplace where people can work together. Important social events such as the Melbourne Cup are celebrated in offices with bites, drinks, even betting. Those who have worked in the public sector for more than 25 years recall the good old days when chicken champagne breakfasts were served during Melbourne Cup Day. Some offices even organise a fancy dress to celebrate occasions. Easter too is another event that may be celebrated at the office with hot cross buns served and shared among colleagues.

Christmas and end-of-the-year office parties are a big celebration for some companies. My husband worked for a consultancy in Melbourne several years ago and was amazed that these celebrations stretched half the day—alcohol and food were almost limitless.

Birthdays, maternity leave and retirement are also celebrated with a morning tea or sometimes even after-dinner drinks or dinner. There is an air of congeniality at the workplace but this does not compromise the professionalism that is demanded at work. Other new residents, who have not grown up in a drinking culture, have developed social drinking in order to fit in. The after-office glass of wine or beer at a pub are a part of fitting in with your colleagues.

LANGUAGE AT THE WORKPLACE

Profanity is accepted at the Australian workplace. This can be quite a rude shock for a timid Asian or polite European. The term "bastard" when used in Australia is most often a term of endearment. Other words which are used to express frustration or humour are also accepted.

While Australians are said to be multicultural and open, you may hear someone referring to a colleague as a "wog", which refers to a person of Mediterranean descent. Interpreting this as racist, you may be surprised to know that Greeks, Lebanese and Italians may refer to themselves as wogs too. So don't be immediately offended if you are referred to as curry or chink—a lot depends on the tone and the context.

Having said that, if you feel that someone is referring to you in a racially derogative manner, you can take this up with the authorities. The Equal Opportunity Act and Federal Legislation offer protection against discrimination.

FAVOURITISM AND CRONYISM

Most Australians would deny that favouritism and cronyism exist in Melbourne as it goes against the Australian sense of fair play. The reality, however, may be different. Speaking with many migrants who have handed in countless application letters, their first break into the workforce is often based on personal recommendation, a connection or a network. While the hiring process will be based on your skills and qualifications, getting that first break may be through word of mouth or a recommendation.

Those who have grown up in Melbourne and attended private schools have the perception that some of their well-connected classmates whose parents are part of the old boys' or old girls' network (parents who had been educated in male-only or female-only private schools and who have social and business connections with their alumni) are better placed to get their first job.

When it comes to climbing the corporate ladder, however, you will need to perform and this works on merit. If you try and curry favour by giving gifts to your boss, this may be misinterpreted as bribery. Just because you are friends with the boss does not mean that you will receive special treatment.

The 2018 saga with the ex-Deputy Prime Minister Barnaby Joyce and his partner Vicki Campion was met with disapproval from the general public because of the perception of favouritism in her obtaining jobs with the Federal Government. These perceptions may have been misplaced but this shows that Australians support a fair go for all.

WORK VALUES AND CULTURE

Being treated with respect is one of the paramount considerations at work. Aside from considerations such as the salary package, work-life balance and job satisfaction, a respectful employer is valued by employees.

The ability to lead and motivate your staff goes a long way to keeping them. Most Australians take a great deal of pride in what they do for a living and would generally be motivated to work hard by such incentives as a competitive salary, benefits, fair and equitable work conditions, and having their work valued.

Australians are known for their work hard, play hard culture. Located at one end of the world, Australians have had to rely on themselves, to develop and create their own products and solutions to meet their needs. You will see this in the workplace, where there is a great sense of innovation and people tend to solve a problem by themselves before asking for help. Speaking with older Australians, I learnt that when Australians were still dependent on the motherland, Britain, for supplies, they were forced to wait for months, even years. This forced them to innovate.

There are also more small businesses or start-ups compared to corporations. Tradespersons are usually self-employed as they get a better work-life balance and are able to manage their time independently. A lot of services and blue-collared work are managed by families and small businesses.

TALL POPPY SYNDROME

The tall-poppy syndrome—people who stand out from the crowd as the "tallest poppy" would get cut down to size— is seen in all spheres of life, especially in the workplace. Golfer Greg Norman explained the syndrome as a jealousy of success. He went on to compare America and Australia: an American would compliment a person driving a sports car as a having a nice car but in Australia, someone would try and scratch it. This syndrome means that there will be people always criticising icons held up a models because in an egalitarian country, playing up your abilities is not promoted.

Paul Hogan, who made Australia famous in the movie *Crocodile Dundee*, was subject to criticism for promoting a stereotype of a chauvinistic Australian male, despite the worldwide popularity of the movie.

Elisa-Marie Dumas, head of partner development and corporate innovation at investment group Investible, described in *Business Insider* how she had to learn to fit into Australian

culture and talk about her achievements in a subtle way in order to build trust. This was in contrast to her time in Silicon Valley where she had to be visible and loud to promote herself.

To young Australians, however, the picture is slightly different. It seems the tall poppy syndrome remains a relic of the past. Hard work and networking is the way to get ahead in your career now, and younger people are open to all who share these values.

VOLUNTEER WORK

Volunteering is big in Melbourne and many people volunteer on a permanent basis. Even people in full-time employment volunteer, and many corporate organisations support their employees in doing volunteer work. In Melbourne, there many organisations which require volunteers, from charities and schools to farms. As a volunteer there are certain rights you enjoy such as a safe working environment, respect from the organisation and freedom from harassment. There are volunteering support organisations that offer guidance. In Melbourne there is Code of Conduct which both organisations and volunteers have to abide by. If you require more information about being a volunteer, visit www.volunteer. vic.gov.au.

For migrants who wish to volunteer, there may be visa requirements from the organisation and you may need to check with the Department of Home Affairs.

Certain sectors such as child care and education require mandatory screening of staff and volunteers, in recognition of the risks and responsibilities attached to the position. The usual checks are character and professional references, driving records, experience working with children and background and police checks. Australia places importance on this screening process and takes steps to protect staff, volunteers and users.

FINDING WORK AS A NON-NATIVE ENGLISH SPEAKING MIGRANT

For those who come from cultures where employability is largely based on paper qualifications alone, you would need to work on your social, oral, presentation and self-branding skills. As part of the preparation you should have considered your strengths and weaknesses, your past experiences and how you would fit the job in terms of responsibilities as well as into the culture of the organisation. In many companies, how you fit into the company culture does matter. Just meeting the selection criteria is not enough. You should never underestimate the unwritten requirements of a job.

If you are struggling to get your first job, it would be good to network with recruitment consultants, headhunters, hiring managers and friends. You could speak to friends who may know of prospective employers. Until you find a job, you should volunteer. It will help you gain experience and give you a sense of value, dignity and self-esteem.

The use of social media as a tool for employers and employees is increasing. Having a professional LinkedIn profile may improve your visibility in terms of getting employment in Melbourne. Hudson Australia which is one of Australia's leading recruitment specialists and provides advice to job seekers on how to use LinkedIn to get a job.

SICKIES

Australians are known for their sickies, a day off when you feel unwell but which does not require getting a medical certificate by a doctor. However, because of the abuse of this custom by some over the years, the sickie is seen as a day off when you have had too much to drink, watched a match overnight, or just don't feel like going to work.

According to an online article by news.com.au, a survey of 500 workers by software company Tsheets found about

40 per cent of workers faked their illness while the remaining 52 per cent were actually sick. The real reasons behind the leave for some were to visit family or friends, to recover from a hangover, attend a job interview or enjoy the good weather at the beach! The article postulated that the sickie culture was due to a sense of entitlement among employees, but also raised that mental health issues such as depression or low job satisfaction could be a factor.

The Fair Work Act 2009 (Cth) prohibits an employer from dismissing an employee due to their temporary absence from the workplace due to sickness or injury. An employee needs to submit a medical certificate or statutory declaration as evidence of their ill health.

Two legal decisions I have come across hinged on the validity of a sickie. In Anderson v Crown Melbourne Ltd (2008), Mr Anderson, an employee of Crown Melbourne and an ardent Essendon supporter, took sick leave to fly to Perth to attend an Essendon match. He provided a doctor's certificate for his absence upon his return, but was dismissed by Crown Melbourne. He then brought a legal action for unfair dismissal, but this failed when the court found that he had been healthy when he applied for the certificate and had planned his trip by first buying the match and plane tickets even before he saw the doctor to obtain the medical certificate.

In another case, Marshall v Commonwealth (2012), the Federal Magistrates' Court held that a medical certificate was valid and ruled in favour of the employee. The facts involved a weather observer, Mr Marshall, who worked with the Bureau of Meteorology. He had been absent from work due to an adjustment disorder but was thereafter certified as medically fit to return to work by the employer's doctor. Mr Marshall obtained another medical report from his own doctor which contradicted the employer's doctor and he was issued a medical certificate. While he was feeling unwell, he wanted to apply for no-pay leave to attend a reality television show. Although he did not take part in the show, his employment was terminated for non-performance. The court found that Mr Anderson's medical report substantiated his illness and the medical certificate issued was valid. Therefore he succeeded in his claim for wrongful dismissal.

PART-TIME AND CASUAL WORK

An employee can be hired as full-time, part-time, or casual. Pay rates, leave and other entitlements such as medical differ with each scheme.

The Fair Work Commission is the Australian industrial relations tribunal created by the Fair Work Act. Its functions include setting and varying industrial awards, minimum wage fixation, dispute resolution, the approval of enterprise agreements, and handling claims for unfair dismissal. It also provides guidelines on pay rates for different industries. There is a branch in Victoria which follows the national system.

Full-time employees work 38 hours per week. A part-time employee works, on average, less than 38 hours per week and is entitled to the same benefits (such as sick leave and holiday leave) as a full-time employee, but on a pro rata basis depending on how many hours they work each week. Casual employees usually work irregular hours but they don't get paid sick leave or annual leave. Check the Fair Work Commission website, www.fwc.gov.au, on these details. Many awards, enterprise agreements and other registered agreements have record-keeping arrangements for part-time employees about their hours of work. Even overtime work is covered by the commission.

Personal Experiences

Candice, an ex-Singaporean living in Melbourne, believes that in Melbourne it's not what you know, but who you know, that first opens the doors to employment. She got her first job as an academic writer through her daughter's school principal. Unlike the popular belief that Aussies are informal and friendly at work, she found them very polite and formal at work. She had only praise for the manner in which the human resources department managed employee welfare, reviews, counselling and feedback.

Rohan, a Sri Lankan migrant who arrived in Melbourne in the early 2000s, had to wait five years before finding a job which suited his human resource skills. In the meantime he settled for casual jobs in retail and hospitality.

Chelsea, a Hong Konger who migrated to Melbourne in the 1980s, found the whole process of getting work as a nurse straightforward. Having had work experience in Britain, it was a smooth transition to nursing in Melbourne. She found the work environment conducive and part-time work was readily available as employers were accomodating and able to meet her specific requests. Towards the early 2000s, she found that nursing was getting more stressful due to the increasing demands of patients and their family.

Sunita, a Malaysian who also migrated to Australia in the 1980s, had a similarly easy transition. Her first job was with a bank in Melbourne. The bank was accommodating and able to meet her request for part-time work. In the banking sector, the work environment has since changed due to increased competition and techological changes.

Bella, a young European with a post-graduate degree from the University of Melbourne found securing full-time employment difficult. Getting a job in the hospitality or retail sector was her best option as there were more opportunities for this sector. Another friend who had worked part-time in the retail and hospitality sectors found the experience largely positive, with good pay and a conducive work environment.

DOS AND DON'TS AT THE WORKPLACE

Do

- Be punctual and professional at work.

- Exchange courtesies with colleagues such as "Good morning" and "How are you doing?"

- Be sincere in your conversations with colleagues by showing an interest but don't be intrusive.

- Refrain from gossip while at work.

- Refrain from using your office computer for personal matters or surfing the internet. If you must do so, do it during your lunch break.

- Make sure your mobile phone is on silent and that you are not constantly looking at your phone during work.

- Remember office emails and other communication should be formal. Use "Kind Regards" or "Sincerely" rather than "Cheers".

- Always use spell check before you send your email out.

- Treat all staff the same regardless of position.

Don't

- Use your mobile phone during work. You can use it during your lunch break.

- Be late for a meeting. Always arrive a few minutes early.

- USE ALL CAPS when sending emails. This sounds like you are yelling.

- Send bulk mass emails. We all love a video of a cat doing something cute but it's a bad idea to forward it to the entire office.

- Engage in public displays of affection such as kissing or touching in the workplace.

- Arrange for a meeting or call your colleague for information on a Friday after 5pm.

CHAPTER 10

FAST FACTS

> **❝Melbourne is wonderfully altered since I last saw it.❞**
>
> **— William John Wills, 1863**

Time

UTC/GMT +10 hours
Daylight Saving Time: +1 hour

Land

Eastern Asia, islands bordering the East China Sea, Philippine Sea, South China Sea, and Taiwan Strait, north of the Philippines, off the southeastern coast of China

Area

City: 37.7 sq km (14.56 sq miles)
Greater Melbourne, incorporating parts of Moorabool Macedon Ranges, Mitchell, Murrindindi Shires, and parts of Yarra Ranges: 9992.5 sq km (3,858 sq miles)

Voltage

Mains voltage in Australia is 230V (50Hz). Appliances from most places in Asia, Africa and Europe work on the same mains voltage, so no need for a voltage converter. Notable exceptions to this are Japan, USA and Canada.

Population

4.9 million (Australian Bureau of Statistics 2017)

Climate

Temperate climate with warm to hot summers, mild springs and autumns, and cool winters.

Ethnic Groups

Greek, Italian, British, Chinese, Indian, Indonesian, African, Korean, New Zealand, Hong Kong, South American, Western European, Eastern European

Major Religions

Christianity, Buddhism, Hinduism, Islam, Judaismn

Government

A federal system based on the Westminster model. There are 3 levels of government, namely, federal, state and local. Melbourne is located in the state of Victoria. Victoria has its own legislature, executive and the judiciary. The Victorian State Government is the executive administrative authority which responsibilities include schools, hospitals, roads and railways, public transport and utilities. Local councils are responsible for community needs such as waste collection, public recreation facilities and town planning.

Currency

Australian dollar (A$ or AUD)

Industries

Professional, scientific and technical, education and training, healthcare and social assistance, finance and insurance, food and beverage, information, media and telecommunications, retail, public administration and construction

Airports

Tullamarine Airport handles international and domestic passengers; Avalon Airport handles domestic passengers.

FAMOUS PEOPLE

Alfred Deakin

Australian politician and second Prime Minister of Australia, Deakin was born in Melbourne. He attended the University of Melbourne and trained as a barrister. At the age of 22, he became a member of the Victorian Legislative Assembly, and subsequently a government minister. Regarded as a founding father by the modern Liberal Party, Deakin contributed to liberal reforms and irrigation development in Australia. In recognition of his contributions, Australia Post issued a postage stamp bearing his portrait in 1969, and Deakin University was established in 1974 as a public university in Victoria.

Barry Humphries (Dame Edna)

A comedian most popularly known as Dame Edna, Humphries was born in Camberwell in 1934. According to him, he escaped what he called "the tremendous emphasis on cleanliness ... and niceness" of Melbourne to roam the world and transform to become the magnificent Dame Edna, superstar and housewife.

Catherine Blanchett (Cate Blanchett)

The multi-award-winning actress and director was born in Ivanhoe, a suburb in Melbourne. She rose to international fame for her role as Elizabeth I of England in the film *Elizabeth* (1998) and received the BAFTA Award for Best Actress and a Golden Globe Award. In 2005 she obtained an Academy Award for Best Supporting Actress for portraying Katharine Hepburn. In 2013, she starred in Woody Allen's *Blue Jasmine*, for which she won the Academy Award for Best Actress.

Chris Hemsworth

The Hollywood actor most popularly known for his role as Thor was born in Melbourne. The middle child in a family of three boys, his childhood was spent both in Melbourne and in the Northern Territory. He recounts, "My earliest memories were on the cattle stations up in the Outback ... probably my most vivid memories were up there in Bulman with crocodiles and buffalo."

Dame Nellie Melba

Born in Richmond, Melba was an Australian opera singer who achieved international fame and was awarded the title Dame of the British Empire in 1918 for raising troop morale in World War I. Her house, Melba Estate, situated in the Yarra Valley, is now a unique gourmet and cultural stop for visitors to the Yarra Valley. She is also the inspiration for the dessert known as "Peach Melba", a dessert of peaches and raspberry sauce with vanilla ice cream, invented by French chef Auguste Escoffier at the Savoy Hotel, London, in honour of her.

Eric Banadinović (Eric Bana)

The Melbourne-born actor began his career as a comedian in the comedy series, *Full Frontal*. Most famously, he played the Hulk in Stan Lee's Marvel Comics film *Hulk* (2003) and Henry De Tamble in *The Time Traveler's Wife* (2009). He received awards from the Australian Film Institute and the Boston Society of Film Critics Award as a member of the best ensemble cast in *Star Trek* in 2009.

Germaine Greer

The world-renowned feminist, writer and academic was born in Elwood, Melbourne in 1939. An arts graduate of theatre, literature and language, she graduated from the

University of Melbourne in 1959 and left for Sydney and then England. She is the author of *The Female Eunuch, Sex and Destiny,* and *The Whole Woman*, and was Professor of English and Comparative Literary Studies at the University of Warwick, England.

Geoffrey Norman Blainey

The infuential Australian historian and academic is the well-known author of *The Tyranny of Distance: How Distance Shaped Australia's History*. His comments on Asian immigration in the 1980s raised much controversy that eventually led to his resignation as Dean of the Faculty of Arts at the University of Melbourne. He has since written other books on Australian history and Christianity. He was made a Companion of the Order of Australia in 2000.

John Farnham

The entertainer spent his first ten years in the United Kingdom before his family emigrated to Australia in 1959 to live in Melbourne. He is one of Australia's most popular performers, and is the only Australian artist to have a number one record in five consecutive decades. Farnham has been recognised by honours and awards including Australian of the Year, Officer of the Order of Australia, 19 ARIA (Australian Recording Industry Association) Awards, and a 2003 induction into the ARIA Hall of Fame.

Kylie Minogue

The international pop star and "Princess of Pop" was born in Melbourne and moved to the United Kingdom in the 1990s. Her singing career has spanned more than two decades, from her humble beginnings in the popular Australian television soap, *Neighbours* to being the highest-selling Australian artist of all time by the Australian Recording

Industry Association (ARIA). She survived a battle with breast cancer in 2005. Internationally, she was awarded the Order of the British Empire for services to music in 2008 and was also presented with the Order of Arts and Letters by the French government for her contribution to the enrichment of French culture.

Keith Rupert Murdoch, AC KCSG

The founder and head of News Corporation, a global media conglomerate, and creator of the Fox Broadcasting Company was born in Melbourne. He is the son of Sir Keith Murdoch and Dame Elisabeth Murdoch and of English, Irish, and Scottish ancestry. An influential yet controversial media figure, he remains a spokesman for Australia.

Mirka Mora

Melbourne's art scene has benefitted from the French artist's talent as she was one of the players who established the Contemporary Art Society in Melbourne from 1953. With her husband, they introduced European-style dining to Melbourne in the 1950s, with the Mirka Café in Exhibition Street, the Balzac in East Melbourne and Tolarno in St Kilda. Her public artwork can be seen at Flinders Street Station (mosaic murals) and St Kilda Pier.

Mark Anthony Philippoussis

The retired tennis player of Greek and Italian descent was born in Melbourne. Nicknamed "The Scud", after the Scud missile, he turned professional in 1994 and his greatest achievements are two Davis Cup titles in 1999 and 2003, winning the deciding rubber in the final of each. He also reached the finals of the 1998 US Open and the 2003 Wimbledon tournaments. He has held a singles ranking of World Number 8.

Ned Kelly

The infamous Australian bushranger and robber was born in Beveridge Victoria and was hung in Melbourne in 1880 at just 25 years old. He was famous for his anti-establishment beliefs and activities. Born into a poor family, he sought a living by thieving and was known to free land owners from mortgages by burning the mortgage deeds while robbing banks. He was sentenced to death by hanging for shooting a police officer, his famous last words were said to be "Such is life".

Peter Carey

Born in Bacchus Marsh in Victoria in 1943, the novelist began his writing career in advertising copy and moved to fiction focused on Australian identity and history. His novel, *Oscar and Lucinda*, on the arrival of Christianity in Australia, won the Booker Prize in 1988. In 2001, *True History of the Kelly Gang* earned him a second Booker Prize. In 2012, he was appointed an Officer of the Order of Australia for distinguished services to literature. He lives in New York and teaches creative writing at New York University.

Rachel Griffiths

The actress and director was born in Queensland but has lived in Melbourne from the age of five and currently resides here. She began her acting career appearing on the Australian series, *Secrets* and had a supporting role in the comedy *Muriel's Wedding* (1994). She gained international recognition for her role opposite Julia Roberts in the American romantic comedy *My Best Friend's Wedding* (1997), and was nominated for an Academy Award for Best Supporting Actress for her role in *Jackie* (1998). For her role in the HBO series *Six Feet Under* (2001 to 2005), Rachel earned a Golden Globe Award for Best Actress.

Shane Warne

Born in 1969 in Upper Ferntree Gully, Victoria, an outer suburb of Melbourne, the former Australian international cricketer was a former ODI captain of the Australian national team. Widely regarded as one of the greatest bowlers in the history of the game, Warne was named one of the Wisden Cricketers of the Year in the 1994, the Wisden Leading Cricketer in the World in 1997 (Notional Winner) and 2004. He is listed as one of the five Wisden Cricketers of the Century. He retired from cricket in July 2013.

Sidney Myer

The Russian migrant came to Melbourne in 1899 virtually penniless. He changed his name from Simcha to Sidney and set up the departmental store known as Myers. The first store was in Bendigo. Myers is today Australia's largest department store which sells a broad range of products from clothes to computers.

Sir John Monash

The Australian military commander of the First World War was born in Melbourne in 1865. In May 1918 he became commander of the Australian Corps and planned with Canadian commander Arthur Currie, a combined Allied Australian and Canadian Corps strategy at the Battle of Amiens on 8 August 1918, which hastened the end of the war. For his war effort, Monash is considered Australia's most famous military commander. He was awarded several awards including the Grand Officer of the Legion of Honour (France), Grand Officer of the Order of the Crown (Belgium), Distinguished Service Medal (United States), Knight Grand Cross of the Order of St Michael and St George, and Knight Commander of the Order of the Bath. He was Vice-Chancellor of the University of Melbourne and a public university, Monash

University, was established in 1958 by an Act of Parliament. His image appears on the A$100 currency note and a cantata for chorus, soloists and orchestra called *Peace – A Cantata for John Monash* was composed by Dr David Ian Kram in his honour in 2008.

Steve Irwin

The world renowned wildlife expert was born in 1962 in Melbourne. He moved to Queensland with his family in early childhood and was nicknamed the "The Crocodile Hunter", achieving worldwide fame from the television series of the same name. He and his wife, Terri Irwin, co-hosted international wildlife documentary series *Croc Files* (1999–2001), *The Crocodile Hunter Diaries* (2002–2006), and *New Breed Vets* (2005). Irwin died in 2006 due to a piercing of his heart by a stingray while he was filming an underwater documentary, *Ocean's Deadliest*.

Tina Arena

Filippina Lydia "Tina" Arena was born in 1967 in Melbourne and is of Italian descent. She is one of Australia's highest selling female artists. Among the awards she has received are seven Australian Recording Industry Association (ARIA) Awards and two World Music Awards for Bestselling Australian Artist in 1996 and in 2000. In 2011, she was awarded a Knighthood of the French National Order of National Merit for her contributions to French culture.

CULTURE QUIZ

SITUATION 1

The whole office is out for drinks at the successful conclusion of a sales agreement. You are a new manager in a large office. You are eager to be accepted and would like to treat everyone to a round of drinks. What is the appropriate conduct?

A Treat everyone to a round of drinks after having introduced yourself.

B Let everyone order and pay for their drinks. Go Dutch.

C Follow the crowd and observe before doing anything.

Comment

Possibly **A** is the best option. Generally it is an Australian custom to shout or buy a round so this is acceptable. However as a new manager, drawing attention to yourself may seem arrogant unless you were involved in the successful contract. **B** is acceptable too depending on the culture of the organisation. **C** is for those who still are green and unaware of the culture, and this is the most prudent option.

SITUATION 2

You are enjoying your first month at work in Melbourne in a small firm. A manager needs help with the software application but the person in charge of IT is on leave. You are competent in IT knowledge and application skills, though your job role is not in IT. What should you do in this situation?

A Wanting to impress the manager, you introduce yourself, explain your prior experience and help solve the problem.

B Offer your help, saying that you are not an expert but are willing to try and solve the problem.

C Keep quiet and suggest that the manager wait until the IT staff is able to help.

Comment

B may be the best option. It would not draw too much attention to yourself and you would not stand out as a tall poppy. **A** is not the best option as you may come across as arrogant. **C** may be seen as unhelpful if the issue is urgent.

SITUATION 3

A neighbour invites you for a meal at their home, together with another pair of neighbours. You want to show your gratitude to the hosts. Is there an appropriate gift to bring?

A A bottle of wine
B Flowers and chocolate
C A plate to share

Comment

Both **A** and **B** are possible options. A bottle of wine, flowers and chocolate are appreciated. However **C** may not be a good option even if well intended, as what you bring may not be in line with the menu for dinner or palatable to the host.

DOS AND DON'TS

DOS
- Smile and say hello when walking in your neighbourhood.
- Refer to someone by their first name.
- Learn about sports, especially AFL, to be able to fit in.
- Learn to go Dutch when dining with others.
- Bring a bottle when you are invited to a party.
- Refer to a colleague's other as their partner to avoid any social awkwardness. All types of relationships are accepted: lesbian, gay, bisexual, trans, and/or intersex.
- Learn the lingo or slang.
- Learn to be handy: There are many DIY tools available at Bunnings, a household name in Melbourne and Australia.
- Take the Australian sun and wind seriously by wearing sun protection and layer up to avoid getting sick.
- Follow local laws and regulations seriously.

DON'TS
- Use Australian slang if you are unaware of the meaning.
- Get easily upset over swearing at work or a social event.
- Speak about sensitive issues such as politics, race or religion at social events.
- Begin a conversation by asking about a person's social status or family background.
- Try to impress with expensive cars, clothes, and possessions.
- Compare Melbourne with your home country.
- Try to impress with your knowledge.
- Cut queue or grumble when having to queue.
- Try and bargain in fixed price shops.
- Overflatter as it may be viewed as insincere.

RESOURCE GUIDE

EMERGENCY CALLS
- **Emergency Fire Police Ambulance**   000 (Freecall)
- **For TTY users (hearing or speech
  impaired)**   106
- **Emergency Services (SES)**   132 500
- **Non Emergency Police**   131 444
- **International Security Hotline**   1800 1234 00
  to report any suspicious activities
  to report on security or terrorism
- **Crime Stoppers**   1800 333 000
  to report crimes that are not in progress

SPECIFIC EMERGENCY NUMBERS
- **Poisons Information Centre (24 hours)**
  131 126
- **Care Ring: 24 hour counselling service**
  136 169
- **Life Line: 24 hour service.**
  131 114
- **Public transport & timetables**
  131 638
- **Accident Towing**
  131 176
- **Dentists: Dental Hospital Service (Emergency Only)**
  9341 1040
- **Maritime and Aviation Rescue**
  9674 3000

VICTORIAN EMERGENCY SERVICES
Gas: Leaks and Emergencies
- **Multinet Gas**
  132 691
- **Envestra**
  1800 676 300
- **AusNet Services**
  136 707

Electricity: Power Failure
- **Citipower**
  13 12 80
- **Powercor**
  13 24 12
- **AusNet Services**
  13 17 99
- **Jemena**
  13 16 26
- **United Energy**
  13 20 99
- **Nurse On Call:**
  1300 606 024 | AMA Victoria's Doctor Search

Animals: Veterinary
- **Melbourne Veterinary Clinic [Werribee]**
  9731 2232
- **Lord Smith Hospital [North Melbourne]**
  9328 3021
  (Source: www.onlymelbourne.com.au)

LISTINGS OF EMBASSIES
The complete list of embassies and consulates in Melbourne can be found at www.onlymelbourne.com.au/consulates-embassies.

HOSPITALS

There are more than 100 hospitals in Victoria. A full list can be found at www2.health.vic.gov.au/hospitals-and-health-services and www.myhospitals.gov.au/browse-hospitals/vic/melbourne/melbourne. Some established hospitals in Melbourne are:

- **The Royal Melbourne Hospital**
  (not for childbirth or children's services)
  300 Grattan Street (corner of Royal Parade)
  Parkville, Victoria 3050
  Telephone: +61 3 9342 70000
- **The Royal Women's Hospital**
  Grattan St & Flemington Rd
  Parkville VIC 3052 AUSTRALIA
  Main Reception: (03) 8345 2000
- **The Royal Children's Hospital**
  50 Flemington Road
  Parkville, Victoria 3052.
  Telephone: +61 3 9345 5522
- **The Royal Victorian Eye and Ear Hospital**
  32 Gisborne Street
  East Melbourne
  Victoria 3002
  Telephone: +61 3 9929 8666

SCHOOLS

The full list of schools in Victoria can be found at
http://www.education.vic.gov.au/school/parents and
https://privateschoolsguide.com/melbourne-private-schools

EXPAT CLUBS

The Maryborough Highland Society was established by Scottish emigrants to promote the music, literature, dancing and games of Scotland. It has its own club house with facilities. It is located at 35 High Street, Maryborough 3465.

GreekCentral.com.au is a unique Greek internet directory for Greeks and non-Greeks alike, ranging from business listings to scheduled Greek-culture-related events.

The Melbourne Lithuanian Club hosts social and cultural events. It has facilities such as a theatre, bar and function rooms. It is located at 44 Errol Street, North Melbourne 3051.

The Chinese Youth Society of Melbourne is a non-profit society which promotes Chinese culture. It is located at Factory 4, 2-4 Joseph Street, Blackburn North 3130.

The German Club Tivoli promotes German culture through activites such as dance, song and language. It is located at 291 Dandenong Road, Prahran/Windsor VIC 3181.

The Canada Club of Victoria is a not-for-profit social club which hosts events such as Thanksgiving dinner and Canada Day Celebrations. The club can be contacted at info@canadaclub-vic.org.au.

The Australian Hispanic Society is a social organisation which promotes Hispanic culture and language. It is located at Box Hill Community Arts Centre, 470 Station Street, Box Hill, VIC 3128.

The Portuguese Association of Victoria promotes appreciation of Portuguese culture. It is located at 201 Palm Springs Rd, Ravenhall 3023.

The Japanese Society of Melbourne, also known as the Australia Japan society, organises events throughout the year for the Japanese community. It is located at 2/99 Queen St, Melbourne VIC 3000.

The American Chamber of Commerce in Australia provides assistance to US and Australian companies and works to promote trade, commerce and investment between Australia and the US. It is located at Southern Cross Tower, International Chamber House, 121 Exhibition St, Melbourne VIC 3000.

The Irish Australian Chamber of Commerce is a business organisation which organises frequent networking and business events in Melbourne. It is located at Level One, 530 Little Collins Street, Melbourne VIC 3000.

RELIGIOUS INSTITUTIONS

There are at least 100 listings for religious organisations in Melbourne. Notable on the list is St Paul's Cathedral (an Anglican cathedral), St Patricks Cathedral (a Catholic Cathedral), Buddhist temples such as the Melbourne Buddhist Centre in Brunswick, Hindu temples such as the Sri Vakrathunda Vinayagar Temple in Basin, mosques such as Fitzroy Mosque and West Melbourne Mosque, Sikh temples in Blackburn and Hoppers Crossing, and Jewish synagogues in East Melbourne.

VOLUNTEER ORGANISATIONS

There is a volunteering portal which provides online resources to volunteers at https://www.volunteer.com.au/volunteering/in-melbourne. Another website https://govolunteer.com.au allows you to choose to volunteer in corporate, event, environment, student and emergency services.

The youth central website, www.youthcentral.vic.gov.au/jobs-and-careers/volunteering-and-work-experience provides a list of arts and media organisations, community support organisations, educational organisations, environmental organisations, health organisations, and social justice organisations to choose from.

BOOKSHOPS

Independent bookstores include Readings in Carlton (which has a collection of travel, design, architecture and history books), The Paperback Bookshop and Hill of Content. The latter is Melbourne's oldest bookstore and is a two-story treasure trove for book lovers. In nearby suburbs, there is the Avenue Bookstore at Albert Park, the Grumpy Swimmer in Elwood, and Coventry bookstore in South Melbourne.

Specialty bookstores include Embiggen books in the CBD where you will find specialist books on design, art, photography and architecture; Metropolis Bookshop located in the CBD (and Melbourne's answer to Kinokuniya); The Little Book Room in Carlton North (a quaint children's bookstore reminiscent of the book shop in the movie, *You've Got Mail*); and Books for Cooks located in the Queen Victoria Market (a specialty store for cooks).

There are second hand bookstores such as Grub Street bookshop in Fitzroy, City Basement Books in the CBD and The Searchers in Fitzroy.

Chain bookstores such as Dymocks in the CBD and the Book Grocer offer wallet-friendly book deals which allow readers to stock up on a decent range of books including Penguin classics.

Bookstore bars are where you can marry your love of books with alcohol. Buck Mulligan's is a book store which serves whisky while Willows & Wine sells pre-loved books and wine.

NEWSPAPERS / MAGAZINES

The Age is available on subscription at theage.com.au. *The Age* is a daily newspaper that has been published in Melbourne since 1854. The newspaper is owned and published by Fairfax Media. Although it is targeted to serve Victoria, it is also available in Tasmania, the Australian Capital

Territory and border regions of South Australia and southern New South Wales. *The Age* is available both in hard copy and online. *The Sunday Age* is popular too.

Herald Sun is a morning newspaper published by The Herald and Weekly Times Ltd, a subsidiary of News Corp Australia, itself a subsidiary of News Corp. The Sunday edition is also popular.

Melbourne City Newspaper is a vibrant free inner city weekly publication which covers a broad range of news, arts, travel, education, food, wine, fashion and sports.

FURTHER READING

- *The Lucky Country.* Donald Horne. Penguin, 2009
- *A History of Victoria*. Geoffrey Blainey. Cambridge University Press, 2013
- *Melbourne, A City of Villages*. Dale Camprisi. Explore Australia Publishing, 2015
- *Melbourne: past and present*. Sheridan Morris. Axiom Australia, 2009
- *Mateship: a very Australian History*. Nick Dyrenfurth. Scribe Publications, 2015
- *Why we are Australian: 125 defining men, women and moments over three centuries*. Paul Taylor. The Five Mile Press, 2007
- *Australia: a survival guide to customs and etiquette*, Ilsa Sharp. Marshall Cavendish Editions, 2009
- *Melbourne then and now*. Heather Chapman and Judith Stillman. Salamander Books Limited, 2014
- *Walking with an Australian hiring manager: what migrants need to know coming to this lucky country*. Kin Kok Low. Partridge Publishing, 2017
- *The story of Australian English*. Kel Richards. New South Publishing, 2015
- *The little book of Australia.* David Dale Allen & Unwin. Crows Nest NSW Australia, 2010
- *Fair Dinkum!: Aussie Slang*. H.G. Nelson. National Library of Australia, 2015
- *Australian Slang.* Penguin Group (Australia), 2008
- *Laneways of Melbourne*. Kornelia Freeman and Ulo Pukk. Melbourne Books, 2013

ABOUT THE AUTHOR

Ruth Rajasingam is a lawyer by training and taught law for the last ten years. Born in Singapore, she first lived in Melbourne in 1998 for a few years and more recently, since 2017 with her family. She enjoys the multicultural lifestyle in Melbourne with its varied cuisine, walks in the parks, and the vibrant sports and arts scenes the city has to offer.

INDEX

Titles in the **CultureShock!** series:

Argentina	France	Philippines
Australia	Germany	Portugal
Austria	Great Britain	Russia
Bahrain	Greece	San Francisco
Bali	Hawaii	Saudi Arabia
Beijing	Hong Kong	Scotland
Belgium	Hungary	Sri Lanka
Berlin	India	Shanghai
Bolivia	Ireland	Singapore
Borneo	Italy	South Africa
Bulgaria	Jakarta	Spain
Brazil	Japan	Sri Lanka
Cambodia	Korea	Sweden
Canada	Laos	Switzerland
Chicago	London	Syria
Chile	Malaysia	Taiwan
China	Mauritius	Thailand
Costa Rica	Morocco	Tokyo
Cuba	Munich	Travel Safe
Czech Republic	Myanmar	Turkey
Denmark	Netherlands	United Arab Emirates
Dubai	New Zealand	USA
Ecuador	Norway	Vancouver
Egypt	Pakistan	Venezuela
Finland	Paris	Vietnam

For more information about any of these titles, please contact the Publisher via email at: genref@sg.marshallcavendish.com or visit our website at:

www.marshallcavendish.com/genref